THE
HAUNTING OF
ASYLUM
49

THE HAUNTING OF ASYLUM 49

×××××××××××××××××××

CHILLING TALES OF AGGRESSIVE SPIRITS,
PHANTOM DOCTORS, AND THE
SECRET OF ROOM 666

×××××××××××××××××××

RICHARD ESTEP
and CAMI ANDERSEN

THE HAUNTING OF ASYLUM 49
EDITED BY ROGER SHEETY
TYPESET BY PERFECTYPE, NASHVILLE, TENN.
Cover illustration by Howard Grossman/12E Design
Printed in the U.S.A.

To order this title, please call toll-free 1-800-CAREER-1 (NJ and Canada: 201-848-0310) to order using VISA or MasterCard, or for further information on books from Career Press.

The Career Press, Inc.
12 Parish Drive
Wayne, NJ 07470
www.careerpress.com
www.newpagebooks.com

Library of Congress Cataloging-in-Publication Data
CIP Data Available Upon Request.

For my friend Gareth "Ace" Gregson, one of the finest men
that I have ever known.
—Richard Estep

x x x

For my husband Kimm, who is never surprised
by what I can accomplish.
—Cami Andersen

x x x

And for the Asylum 49 family, whether living or dead,
without whom this book could not have been written.

ACKNOWLEDGMENTS

Special thanks are due to our spouses, Laura and Kimm, for taking care of the real world while we were oblivious at our keyboards.

Thanks are also due to the people who make Asylum 49 what it is: Dusty and Lyle Kingston, Sonja Andersen, Misty Grimstead, Ray and Cathy Blank, Tyson and Julie Lemmon, and Robert "Buck" Helige. Thanks to the Utah Ghost Organization who got Asylum 49 started down this crazy road, Troy and Kris Wood, Trudy Roberts, and Dan Roberts. Last, but not least, to the *huge* cast and volunteers of Asylum 49, past and present; the list is far too long to mention everyone, but you all know who you are.

A special thank-you to Travis Shortt, who is always willing to lend his expertise to an old friend.

The investigation would not have been nearly as thorough without the help of Sean Rice, Jason Fellon, Catlyn and Greg Keenan, Randy Schneider, Robbin Daidone, Jennifer Roderick, and Autumn Kingry, all of whom traveled a long way in pursuit of their desire to investigate the paranormal.

Thank you all. We couldn't have done it without you!

CONTENTS

FOREWORD

My room was filled with visitors and medical staff alike, all stopping by to check on my recovery after an emergency gallbladder removal. The pain was unreal and I was connected to a wonderful pain reduction system (morphine drip), and with the push of a button could control my own pain/pleasure principle and control it—or perhaps over control it—I did. That is when I started to notice a very strange situation unfolding in my hospital room; I realized that aside from the busyness of visitors and nurses checking on me, I had, unbeknownst to the others in my room, a large gathering of shadowy figures watching over me, patiently waiting for those moments when I would see them and they could attempt communication.

Now I know what you are all thinking: drugs, hallucinations, wild imagination. And I cannot for certain disagree. However, I know that those moments, when I could see them, are burned in my memory more clearly than the conversations and interactions I was having with my living, breathing visitors.

Never before had I experienced such a strange and surreal situation. While my eyes were open, I could see, hear, and communicate with all of my fleshy, warm-blooded friends; when my eyes closed, I could still see every detail of my room, with the exception of the actual people in it. I could still hear them and interact, but they were no longer in my visual spectrum. Instead, my room was filled with ashen-faced, silent beings, many of whom stood there, watching me, and only a few would move. Then there was The

Woman, a wild-haired, elderly woman who would float there in front of my face, her hair seemingly blown by some unseen force, her eyes piercing, and her face filled with lines and anguish. She would stare deeply into my eyes, screaming words I could not hear, insisting that I pay attention to her. She grew angrier and more persistent as my stay continued, which also led me to believe that this was more, so much more, than a drug-fueled hallucination. My consciousness, or perhaps subconsciousness, was wide open to another level of existence and they knew it; they could sense that I was straddling two realms and they were opportunists, making sure that I would see and remember everything.

In the days after I was released, I wracked my brain trying to understand, often vacillating between belief and disbelief of what it was I witnessed. I tried so hard to convince myself that everything I saw and experienced was the machination of a drug-induced haze, but I could remember it all so clear, so vivid, and that stuck with me.

That sent me down a rabbit hole that I have yet to pull myself out of, trying to understand or comprehend what is going on around us, unseen at all times. Are we just that close to another reality or dimension? Do the dead really surround us? Then my heart sank as I thought about a room full of ashen, washed-out ghosts, trapped, caught between this world and the next, and filling the rooms and halls of hospitals, asylums, and institutions around the world. How many millions or hundreds of millions of spirits must still walk their halls?

What I found most disturbing was why they were still here, walking among us, especially in places like that. I would hope that in the end, if I stay, I will be bouncing between visiting my kids, scaring some investigators at Asylum 49, or popping in and out of the Minnesota Vikings Cheerleaders' dressing room. (What? Hey, I am only human.) Why do spirits choose to stay or be stuck in these circumstances? My only solace came from a fellow investigator and researcher who shed some light on what may come next and why those who stay are still here.

Miss Bay looked deeply into my eyes and said:

> When we die, all that we are, all the good, the promise, the light, will go on and complete its journey. Wherever that may be and that

which is left behind is the anger, the resentment, jealousy, pettiness, the base, the animal part of all of us. That is why communication is often short and limited to bangs, flickering lights, and an occasional "GET OUT" and why most communication is so basic. It leaves behind the animal instinct, the pack mentality of sticking with others like itself in an environment that it is familiar with, until at some point that energy fades and finally goes out like a match in a breeze.

I looked at her and questioned, "Then what happens to the light of us, the best of us?"

Without missing a beat, she lifted the beer bottle to her lips, took another long pull off of it, and said, "Now that is the *real* question, isn't it?"

With that we sat in silence enjoying our libations and reflecting on the imaginings of what lies beyond.

Try to comfort yourselves with that thought as you enter Asylum 49 and read about the spirits, the communication, and the reality that seems to be pushing itself into our realm. Take a moment to realize that, much like Jacob Marley warned in *A Christmas Carol*, the chains we forge in this life we must carry on to the next. Be kind, shorten those chains, and make life right while you have the chance, instead of leaving a dark and tortured version of yourself behind, bonded to this Earth by all the negativity we create for ourselves and bask in daily. Maybe the longer you allow the negative in and to surround you, the longer that part of you will stay behind until it fades.

Welcome to a world of possibilities, of nightmares, and hope. Welcome to the reality that is *The Haunting of Asylum 49*.

Dave Schrader
Host of *Darkness Radio* and guest host of *Coast to Coast AM*.

INTRODUCTION

What you are about to read is the culmination of many hours of paranormal research, conducted by a great number of men and women, during the space of almost 10 years.

If this true story has a central character, then that character has to be the old Tooele Valley Hospital, located just outside Salt Lake City. Through the course of its lifetime as not only a hospital, but also as a haunted house attraction, thousands of people have laughed and cried inside its walls, as the building served as a stage for the full spectrum of human drama.

Along with intense emotion, of course, one usually finds ghosts, and the former hospital (now better known by the name of Asylum 49) is no exception. The idea of a haunted hospital is hardly a unique one, but what *is* unique is the fact that ever since the building passed into private hands, the owners, staff members, and more recently several teams of paranormal investigators, have spent hundreds of nights in the process of delving into the truly stunning array of phenomena that are said to take place there.

We (the authors) are well aware of the extraordinary nature of some of those claims. As we interviewed witness after witness, we were subjected to a barrage of increasingly spectacular stories that involved phantom children, malevolent dark masses, and spectral doctors that caused us to raise our eyebrows more than a few times; yet each observer calmly, but resolutely, stuck to their guns when cross-examined, impressing us with their sincerity and determination to share their story, no matter how bizarre and unusual their stories may have sounded.

Both of us have experienced paranormal phenomena at Asylum 49 ourselves, and are in no doubt as to the reality of the haunting. What fascinates us both most of all is twofold. Firstly, we are deeply interested in the spiritual cast of characters that are still in residence at the Asylum, and we hope to share their backstories with a wider audience. We are also curious as to exactly *why* the place is such a hotbed of paranormal activity, with visitors and staff reporting ghostly encounters on an almost daily basis.

This book could not have been written without the many people who generously gave their time and shared their stories with us, and we are extremely grateful for their willingness to come forward and recount their paranormal experiences for inclusion in the book.

We would be most remiss, however, if we did not thank the spirits of Asylum 49 themselves, without whom there would *be* no book in the first place.

We hope you enjoy reading their stories as much as we have enjoyed documenting them.

Richard Estep and Cami Andersen

1

Birth of an Asylum

For as long as he could remember, Kimm Andersen had always been fascinated with haunted houses.

It wasn't the historic, spooky old mansion whose corridors were prowled by ghostly ladies in white that Kimm would end up devoting his life to, however; he was far more interested in the theatrical variety, the sort of haunted house that you could take your family to at Halloween and, after handing over a few bucks for the privilege, give them the scare of their life in a safe (yet also creepy) house of horrors.

This love for the haunted house scene (such places are known simply as "haunts" to those in the profession) went all the way back to his youth. Following a spur-of-the-moment decision one night, the teenage Kimm wandered into his local haunt and asked if he could get involved somehow. Before he knew what was happening, he found himself dressed in rags and painted up as a blood-splattered zombie, then placed in a fake graveyard along with several very realistic latex ghoul props and a couple of other performers.

Kimm spent the rest of the night clawing his way out of the ground, moaning and groaning in the manner of the flesh-eating zombies that he had seen in horror movies, eliciting scream after scream from the nervous but eager customers.

It didn't take long for Kimm to realize that he had caught the haunt bug in a major way. He returned the following night, and then every night for the rest of that Halloween season. The next year, when October rolled around once again, he was the first in line to sign up. Seeing his enthusiasm and recognizing his potential, the owners of the haunt offered this enthusiastic teenage boy an expanded role in its day-to-day operation. Soon he was helping to construct and create the haunt in addition to simply performing in it, picking up some basic carpentry and crafting skills along the way.

By the time that the second season was over, Kimm had constructed almost half of the entire haunted house attraction with his own hands.

"Getting involved with that haunt turned my life around," Kimm says. "I wasn't necessarily on the straight and narrow as a kid at that point, and things could have taken some pretty nasty turns if I hadn't been lucky enough to step through that doorway when I did."

Recognizing the many positive ways in which working in a haunt had benefited his own life, Kimm was always looking out for a way to bring those same benefits to others—particularly children and teenagers who were in need of the same break that he had been offered at their age.

Twenty years later, he would finally get his chance. Unbeknownst to Kimm, however, *this* particular haunted house came with its own ghosts and they would turn out to be very, *very* real.

x x x x x

Pulling into the parking lot of the hospital, Kimm took a minute to walk around the exterior and gather his thoughts. The hospital was built on a hill, like all good haunted houses in Hollywood movies seem to be, with a tall smokestack looming above the structure like some kind of sentinel.

As he strolled along the dark and dusty corridors in the company of the realtor who was charged with selling the place, Kimm's mind was hard at work conjuring up images of the haunt that could be built here. The place just *looked* eerie, and that was before anything had been done to it.

When the hospital had closed down four years before, the doctors, nurses, and the small army of support personnel responsible for its upkeep had simply upped and left the place for the last time, locking the doors

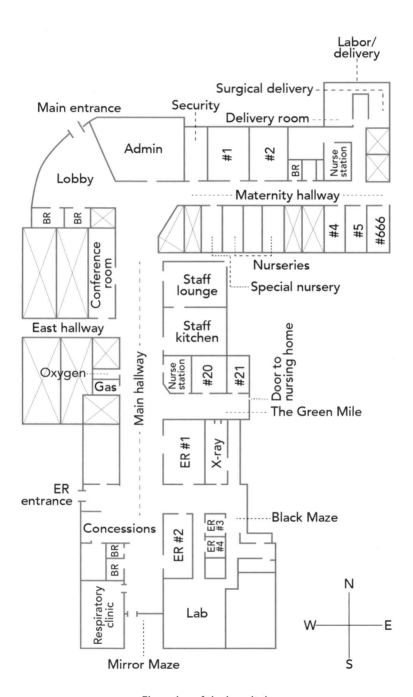

Floor plan of the hospital.

behind them and turning out the lights. They had left behind almost all of the medical equipment that had been a crucial part of the hospital's everyday working life: As Kimm poked his head into the rooms where thousands of patients had lived and died through the years, he was amazed to see rows of hospital beds and oxygen tanks, not to mention actual x-ray films left posted on the walls alongside drawers full of old medical books and training manuals.

It was like walking through a hospital on the day of the apocalypse, he thought to himself; a house of healing where all of the patients and staff had simply . . . gone.

It was *perfect*.

Within weeks, the paperwork was signed, and it was a done deal. Kimm was the proud new owner of the old Tooele Valley Hospital. Along with his sister, plus his niece Dusty and her husband, his plan was to turn it into the most terrifying haunt in the country.

Inklings of the paranormal activity that would soon plague the building cropped up on the very first day of ownership.

Kimm wasn't the first to conceive of using the hospital as a haunt, however; the owner of the nursing home, which is directly connected to the rear of the hospital, had tried running a small haunted house attraction of his own, and the conference room still contained the residue of that particular venture. Long white curtains were draped over wooden beams, running from ceiling to floor in the still and empty room. This formed a cheap but effective maze of sorts, where visitors would claw their way blindly through the white drapes in order to find their way out.

As he pushed the first set of curtains aside and made his way through the corridors of the fabric maze, Kimm started to develop a sense of deep foreboding. Goosebumps flared up across the surface of his skin, and he could feel his heart starting to beat faster and faster. The hairs on the back of his neck prickled. Kimm's body was trying to tell him that he was in the presence of someone—or some*thing*—that his eyes could not see.

Trying to write off what he saw as being a totally irrational fear, ascribing it to the mind games caused by his being sightless inside the maze, he nevertheless hastened to get through the thing as quickly as possible. Something about the place just didn't feel right.

Suddenly, Kimm felt something touching him on the outside of his leg. Sweat beaded his forehead as he slowly craned his neck to look down at his cargo shorts. The growing sense of anxiety now gave way to full-blown fear as he watched the leg of his shorts being tugged by some kind of invisible force.

"Screw this!" For the first time since his childhood, Kimm Andersen turned his back on something that scared him and bolted, flying headlong through the maze. He shoved armfuls of white fabric to either side of him as he struggled to escape.

Back outside in the cold light of day, reason and rationality tried to take over. *Maybe you were just hallucinating,* Kimm tried to tell himself; but deep down, he simply wasn't buying it. Those had been fingers tugging at his shorts . . . tiny little fingers, as though an invisible child was playing with him or trying to attract his attention.

Construction work ramped up during the next few weeks, as the last days of summer gave way to the first days of fall. The Halloween season was fast approaching, and they needed to have a haunt ready to go before October arrived.

The main entrance of Asylum 49.

Kimm avoided the conference room whenever he could, but continued to build sets in the other rooms of the old hospital too. He had a full-time day job as a service advisor for a car dealership, so the only time he had to build was at night or on the weekends. He made a secret vow to only enter the white maze during the daytime, and even then he swore never to go in alone.

The touch of those invisible fingers still frightened him, lingering in the back of his mind.

During this time everyone was having strange experiences. Props would fall off ladders on a regular basis. Tools would disappear after being set down carefully, despite there being nobody in the area that could possibly have moved them. The missing tools would show up later, usually somewhere on the other side of the hospital. When the construction crew was quizzed about the disappearances, nobody admitted to being responsible. It happened far too frequently for it to be the work of a single practical joker.

Then the voices started to be heard. They were sometimes indistinct, but at other times they were clearly heard calling out the names of those working hard to turn the abandoned hospital into a viable haunt. Disembodied bangs and knocks disturbed the Andersens and their volunteers both day and night. Doors would open and close of their own volition, with no apparent rhyme or reason to the activity.

People would see things out of the corner of their eye. Despite their best efforts to try and prevent the bizarre and irritating things that were happening by deliberately placing their tools in flat, stable locations from which they couldn't possibly fall without help, they *still* continued to fall, as though invisible forces were openly defying the owners and their crew of local residents who volunteered to help build the haunt with them.

October arrived, and the haunt—now going by the name of Asylum 49— was starting to take shape; but the tools still fell and vanished, and the voices still came out of nowhere, echoing along the empty hallways. The bangs and knocks still sounded when there was nobody around to create them.

"None of us wanted to look crazy in front of the others," Kimm explains, looking back on those early days with a rueful shake of his head, "so the experiences just weren't talked about. We learned very quickly to place our work tools anywhere but above our heads, because they would most likely fall on top of us if we didn't. We listened to loud music in order to drown out the voices and bangs that were going on all around us. As Halloween got nearer, the activity got worse and worse."

For obvious reasons, Kimm hadn't mentioned the terrifying encounter in the conference room to anybody else, even his own family. One day, as he was walking through the hospital with one of the owners of the connected nursing home, the pair arrived at the entrance to the white fabric maze.

"What do you think of this room?" the owner asked off-handedly.

Trying to act casual, Kimm hesitated at first, but finally caved and decided to come clean about his experience. Bracing himself for ridicule, he was surprised at the response that the owner gave him.

"When we ran our own little haunted house in here last year," the owner began, fixing Kimm with a level stare, "the customers always told us about the very same thing happening in that room."

Almost hesitant to open a can of worms, but at the same time morbidly curious, Kimm asked: "What *exactly* did they say?"

"They'd say that the little blond girl hiding in the middle of that maze was scary as all hell," the owner chuckled, shaking his head. "We never had the heart to tell them that there *wasn't* a little blond girl in there; we didn't have one on staff. I'd put it all down to people seeing things, only they all described her the exact same way. Pretty weird, huh?"

"Yeah," Kimm agreed absently, lost in his own thoughts. "Pretty weird."

He reached out and firmly pulled the conference room door shut. The rest of the tour passed in a blur. Although the nursing home owner made polite conversation, Kimm didn't really hear another word he said. His mind kept coming back to the image of a young girl with blond hair, wondering whether she had been the owner of the little fingers that had reached out to tug at him in the center of that very maze.

x x x x x

The first order of business for any reputable paranormal investigator is to research the background of the supposedly haunted location. This does not simply mean the history of the house or building as it presently stands; it also extends backward in time to cover the land itself, the local environs, and the community that surrounds it.

A skein of death runs through the recorded history of Tooele County. During the 19th century, it was home to the Goshute Native American Tribe. In 1849, the first white settlers, which were members of the LDS (Latter-day Saints) emigration group that had arrived in 1847, established permanent roots in the Tooele Valley.

It wouldn't be long before the new arrivals began to clash with the native Goshutes. The settlers accused the tribespeople of cattle rustling, which served as a justification for them to carry out attacks on the Goshute camps. Much blood was shed, lives were lost on both sides, and the conflict threatened to escalate out of control, until finally a U.S. Bureau of Indian Affairs representative named Robert B. Jarvis convinced some of the nomadic bands to congregate at a reservation named Deep Creek. The negotiations looked promising at first, but when Jarvis resigned in 1860, support for the project disappeared along with him, until finally the reservation was abandoned. Jarvis's replacement, Benjamin Davies, noted that the Goshutes had lost faith in the federal government, and recommended limiting further encroachments on Goshute land. His suggestions were largely ignored, a decision which would serve only to hasten the downward spiral into violence.

Twenty-two overland stagecoach outposts were built on Goshute territory, often on the sites of rare natural springs. Goshute attacks on mail outposts escalated in 1860, resulting in dozens of deaths in alternating waves of raids. At the outbreak of the American Civil War, federal troops left the area in order to participate, entrusting its defense into the hands of the Nauvoo Legion. The settlers set up lookout points and constructed tall mud walls near the site on which Asylum 49 stands today in order to deter Native attacks; they only needed to hold out until military reinforcements arrived in Salt Lake City from California in 1862.

The reinforcements were commanded by General Patrick O'Connor, an officer known to harbor no love for the Native population. O'Connor adopted a ruthless zero-tolerance policy toward the Goshute people. His soldiers attacked Native American camps at will, and the killing was often indiscriminate. A peace treaty was signed in 1863, which included an annuity of goods and 1,000 dollars paid in compensation, given in exchange for an end to the hostilities and the right of free passage through the Native territories.

Two ambulances are permanently stationed outside in the parking lot.

The Great Salt Lake Desert (now more commonly known as the Salt Flats) comprises much of the northern portion of Tooele County, and provided a major stumbling block for the ill-fated Donner-Reed Party in 1846. Its salt-encrusted sand slowed the group's wagons to such an extent that they spent six days crossing its 80-mile length, severely sapping their limited supplies of food and water. The going was hot, dry, and sticky. Many of the wagons became stuck in the thick mud, leaving the travelers with no other choice but to abandon them. Many of the oxen that were harnessed to the wagons also died, as did some of the cows. The end result was the death of several members of the party, which would conclude with the few survivors resorting to cannibalism in order to survive the ordeal.

After the hardships of initial settlement were behind it, Tooele County fast became known as a mining community, and people flocked to its land with dreams of striking it rich during the great gold rush. Silver, salt, copper, and gold mines were all afflicted with countless fires, mining accidents, vio-lent death, and the ever-present scourge of disease.

Once many of the prospects had been mined dry, the mining activ-ity slowed to a near-standstill. Stepping into the void left by the cessation of industrial activity, the U.S. government built several military bases and chemical weapons facilities in Tooele County during the 20th century. The influx of service personnel and their families mandated that a modern hospi-tal should be built to accommodate their healthcare needs.

This would of course turn out to be the Tooele Valley Hospital, but that was not the first such building in town.

There are several different stories surrounding the genesis of the original Tooele Hospital, and it is often difficult to separate fact from fiction when trying to decide between them. Even the local residents have differing ver-sions of which building was the first make-shift hospital in town, but one theme is consistent throughout: the palpable excitement of having a real hos-pital of their very own, one that would serve the needs of the people of Tooele through good times and bad.

Tales are told of surgeries being performed in a building no bigger than an ordinary house, inside rooms that are the size of a modern-day bedroom; babies were commonly born at home, often on living room and kitchen floors, and house calls were the standard way of seeing a doctor if you needed one.

The Tooele Valley Hospital was the first truly modern, state-of-the-art hospital that Tooele had ever seen. Construction on the great building began in 1949, and the facility was opened with great fanfare in 1953.

The residents of Tooele believed that they were getting a facility that would drastically improve the standard of public healthcare. Most of the time, they were given exactly what they expected; nevertheless, according to anecdotal evi-dence, some local residents would later come to dub it the "hospital of death," and chose to travel further afield to Salt Lake City in order to be treated.

It is important to remember that medical science was considerably less sophisticated during the 1950s than it is today. Despite the less than stellar reputation that it had acquired in some quarters, the Tooele Valley Hospital was still staffed with good people, who were delivering the very best patient care that they could manage, often under very difficult circumstances. The hospital's reputation may have been unfairly maligned.

The hospital stayed in operation until it became apparent that its infrastructure was becoming too outdated and its resources too limited to accommodate the needs of a population that was burgeoning, due largely to inexpensive housing that was being constructed in the area. A brand new hospital was soon built, and the old hospital was sadly allowed to wither on the vine, being slowly phased out until it closed its doors for the final time in 2002—as a hospital, at least.

Parts of the sprawling old building were repurposed as a nursing home, but the remainder was allowed to languish, left only under the watchful eyes of its many resident ghosts.

x x x x x

The mysterious phenomena that were being experienced by the construction crew at Asylum 49 were never far from Kimm's mind. He thought about them often, along with the tiny little fingers clutching at him in the white maze. When a local team of paranormal investigators requested permission to spend a night inside the building in an attempt to gather evidence, it was an offer that he was unwilling to turn down.

If Kimm had been expecting the visiting ghost hunters to have a quiet night, then he was to be very much mistaken.

"We have a *boatload* of EVPs," the lead investigator told him excitedly a few nights after their visit.

"EVPs? What are those?" Kimm asked, having never heard the term before.

"EVPs are electronic voice phenomena," the investigator explained patiently. "We use a tape recorder or digital voice recorder in an empty room, then set it to recording and invite any spirits that might be present there to speak and make themselves known to us."

Holy crap, thought Kimm, *voices from thin air? That's pretty wild.*

"And do they?" he wanted to know.

"Sure. But what we tend to hear are random words or phrases, not necessarily making any kind of sense. The ones we recorded at *your* place are amazing!" the investigator practically gushed. "They're fully lucid, intelligent, sometimes even responding directly to our questions. Heck, one of them was the sound of a little girl's voice! You have *got* to let us come back again to investigate further—please?"

That was fine with Kimm. Although it freaked him out a little to think that there might be discarnate entities actually haunting his haunt, he was equally curious to find out about their backstory. Were these spirits earth-bound because of some tragedy that they had experienced within the walls of the old hospital, or were they perhaps returning to the place where they had worked during their physical lifetime?

As he left the building that night and locked the doors behind him, Kimm strolled across the parking lot toward his car, all the time pondering the meaning of those spirit voices. Pulling out into the street, he turned left past the town cemetery. A sudden thought struck him: Could some of the ghosts be visitors from the graveyard, dropping in to poke around the closest concentration of light and life?

The city cemetery sits next door to the Asylum. Could it be responsible for some of the paranormal activity that takes place?

Could it also be possible that some of them died in the hospital, and their bodies were buried in the ground next door? The thought sent a shiver down his spine, and he quickly drove away into the night, leaving the neat rows of marble tombstones behind him.

Ever since his first experience in the maze, Kimm had found it increasingly difficult to believe that Asylum 49 *wasn't* haunted; but he was a skeptical man by nature, and so as he listened to some of the EVPs that the paranormal investigators played back for him, his first response to the sometimes extraordinary sounds was: *Could they have faked all this?*

He soon came to the conclusion that fraud was extremely unlikely. Doing a little behind-the-scenes research on the team, he discovered that they had a respectable pedigree, and a solid reputation among the paranormal research community. They had a quarter of a century's worth of experience in investigating cases like this, in locations that ranged from private residences to industrial facilities, and were one of Utah's first ever teams who did what they did.

Not wanting to turn the keys to his pride and joy over to complete strangers, Kimm had followed the investigators around, maintaining a discreet distance, but also keeping a careful eye on how they went about their business. He was impressed with what he saw, particularly their air of general professionalism during the various experiments that they conducted. This was no bunch of teenage thrill-seekers; rather, they were two pairs of married couples, seasoned researchers who had level heads set on their shoulders. Try as he might, Kimm could uncover no whiff of fraudulence about them, which on the one hand came as a great relief, but on the other was also rather perplexing.

There was only one way to be sure, however, and so the next day, Kimm went out and purchased his own digital voice recorder.

If you can't beat them, join them, he figured, which is how Kimm came to find himself locked inside his own building late one night in February, all alone—except for whichever spirit entities might be locked in there with him.

He didn't really know the first thing about the tradecraft of investigating, but Kimm had at least watched the visiting ghost hunters going about their work, and that provided him with a good starting point. Armed only with a flashlight and the digital voice recorder, he made sure that the exterior doors were properly secured against any unwanted living guests, and set about going in search of the dead ones.

Where to start? Kimm pondered the question while prowling the dark and shadow-filled hallways for inspiration. After wandering around for a while, he finally settled upon the Labor and Delivery ward as the scene of his first solo investigation. So many lives had begun in that place, he reasoned, and sadly more than a few had ended there as well, when babies and sometimes also their mothers were tragically lost during the bloody miracle that is childbirth.

Kimm sat down on the carpeted floor against the half wall of the nurses' station, fired up his recorder, and started asking questions. Despite the fact that it was pitch black in there, the atmosphere was tranquil and didn't feel at all sinister. In fact, he felt as though he could quite easily have curled up and drifted off to sleep. The air felt cold and was almost completely quiet, broken only by the popping of the old boiler pipes that were carrying just enough heat to the radiators to keep the water pipes from freezing during the winter months, and the slow *drip-drip-drip* of one of the porcelain sinks that was located between the pair of delivery rooms.

"Is there anybody here who would like to talk to me?" Kimm asked, feeling faintly ridiculous at talking to thin air.

"Are you male or female?"

Silence.

"What is your name?"

Silence.

"How old are you?"

Silence.

"Are you . . . *were* you a patient here? What about a doctor or a nurse at this hospital?"

Silence.

"Why are you here?"

Kimm continued in this same vein for several more minutes, without any appreciable result. Then, gathering up all of the courage he possessed, he got ready to break a recently made vow.

Getting slowly to his feet, Kimm reluctantly made his way down the long maternity hall and around the corner off the main hallway. When he got to the double wooden doors of the conference room, he began to grow uneasy as his mind went back to the terrifying experience he had in there months earlier, in its earlier incarnation as the white maze. The visiting ghost hunters had recorded the voice of a little girl in there, which made the manner in which his shorts had been tugged make a lot more sense; as a father himself, Kimm knew that small children often tugged at your clothing in that very same way when they wanted your attention, which reassured him slightly.

There's nothing to fear from a child, he told himself again and again as he edged warily into the dust-filled conference room. He had three kids of his own, after all, so surely he ought to be able to handle a dead one . . . right?

He walked in and sat down in one of the vinyl chairs surrounding the large rectangular conference table that dominated the room and started asking questions. He wanted to contact the little blond girl that had tugged at his shorts, and hopefully find out a little about her backstory.

"Is there a little girl here who would like to talk to me?" Kimm asked tentatively, setting the recorder down carefully on top of the empty wooden table.

Silence was his only answer. He carried on with the same list of questions that he had asked in Labor and Delivery, allowing the recorder to run on for another quarter of an hour.

Nothing stirred in the darkness of the conference room. It felt a great deal less sinister in there now that the maze had been taken down, and he was almost able to relax. Almost.

So, where next? Kimm asked himself, after the 15-minute session was up. The paranormal investigators had said that they had gotten some of their more impressive EVPs in the vicinity of what had once been the Emergency Room, so he decided that it would be as good a place as any to chance his luck.

Kimm reasoned that the Emergency Room would have seen more than its fair share of deaths during the course of the hospital's 50 years of operational service. It had two major trauma bays, where the true life-and-death resuscitations would have been worked on by teams of doctors, nurses, and technicians; there were also two smaller patient examination rooms set off to one side for the less-urgent cases, and also narrow side hallways that led to the x-ray department and to the lab.

A large bed occupied the center of the room, surrounded by curtains and cupboards on all sides. Above it hung a huge spotlight mounted on a multidirectional segmented arm. Apart from the ever-present coating of dust that pervaded much of the abandoned equipment, the speckled grey and white tile floor was spotlessly clean, as were all of the sinks and surfaces. It was as though the ER staff had simply put down their stethoscopes, turned off the cardiac monitors, and just walked out . . . which essentially they *had*.

Having made his way past the triage desk and into the middle of the first trauma bay, Kimm simply stood there for a few minutes, just looking around and taking in the ambience. It took little effort to imagine this place in its heyday. He could picture the emergency medical technicians (EMTs) and paramedics bursting through the double doors, wheeling critically-ill patients in on gurneys. Sometimes, an EMT would be riding the rail, pumping hard and fast on the dying trauma victim's chest in an attempt to restore life to their broken and bleeding body.

They would have been met by the on-duty doctors and nurses, who would in turn help the medics slide the patient over from the gurney onto the very bed that Kimm now rested a hand upon, and then calmly and professionally go about the serious business of trying to drag a human life back from the brink of death.

If these walls really could talk, Kimm found himself wondering, *what stories could they tell?*

Time to find out.

Kimm activated the digital voice recorder and launched into his spiel of questions again. Wanting to be thorough, he repeated the same process again and again, beginning in Trauma Bay One, then again in Trauma Bay Two, before finishing up in the two side rooms.

Except for the sound of his soft voice and the dripping of a faucet in the background, the old hospital remained deathly silent.

Kimm checked his watch and sighed. It was getting late and he was starting to think talking to nothing or no one was a waste of his time. He would have been lying if he'd said he wasn't disappointed; despite the fear factor, he had genuinely hoped to experience *something* paranormal that night, but it simply wasn't to be.

Locking the hospital up tightly and setting the alarm for the night, Kimm got into his car and headed home. He lived in a small farming town named Erda, located just on the outskirts of Tooele. The drive afforded him enough time to listen to some of the audio file playback, and so as he pulled out of the Asylum 49 parking lot, it was with the digital voice recorder speaker pressed tightly up against his ear, its tinny chirps competing with the noise of the engine on the near-deserted roads.

As question after question was met with no intelligible response, Kimm's heart began to sink. Maybe the paranormal investigators had some special abilities that he just didn't possess; or maybe, he thought darkly, they really *had* faked the voices on their own recordings.

The miles passed by along with the repeated questions. Almost before he knew it, he was listening to the segment that had been recorded in Emergency Room Three, the first of the two smaller examination rooms.

"Is there anybody here who would like to talk to me?" Kimm heard his own voice asking.

"*I'm dyin'!*"

Involuntarily, Kimm slammed on the brakes. The car came to a halt with a screech of brakes. Scrabbling for the rewind button, Kimm went back 10 seconds and played the same stretch of recording again.

"*I'm dyin'!*"

It was scratchy, especially when heard over the hissing voice recorder speaker, but it was quite plainly a deep male voice . . . and it was responding directly to *him*.

Kimm could feel his heart pounding inside his chest. He had been all alone in the Emergency Room, that much could not be disputed; in fact, with the doors and windows all secured, he was all alone in the entire *building*. Nobody had spoken aloud during any of his recording sessions, of that he was utterly certain.

"Oh my God," Kimm whispered to himself. "It really *is* real. It really is . . ."

2

All Hallows' Eve

Although it sounds like something straight out of a pulp horror novel, dark storm clouds really were gathering in the sky above the old Tooele Valley Hospital when paranormal investigator and author Richard Estep pulled into the parking lot of Asylum 49 for the very first time.

It had been a long cross-country drive from Colorado to Utah—close to 500 miles, door to door—but Estep and his fellow investigators Jason Fellon and Sean Rice had made it in a little under nine hours. The sunny springtime weather of Boulder County had been replaced with a low grey overcast ceiling, which threatened torrential rain at any moment, and reminded Richard fondly of his native England.

Contracted by a publisher to write his latest book (*The World's Most Haunted Hospitals*), Richard had heard about the many ghost stories that surrounded Asylum 49, and found himself intrigued not only by the volume of accounts, but also by their sheer diversity.

Even a brief Internet search revealed that the place attracted visitors (particularly paranormal investigators) like bees to honey. Before venturing out, the three Coloradans had watched the episode of *Ghost Adventures* in which Zak Bagans and his team had spent the night on lockdown there, which culminated in an apparent attack on Bagans by the ghost of a patient who was known to behave violently in one of the rooms there. Bagans appeared to be shoved aggressively backward by an invisible force after deliberately provoking the spirits in an attempt to gain a response, a true case of "be careful what you wish for" if ever there was one.

Seeking more haunted hospital locations to cover, the writer reached out to the owners of Asylum 49 to see whether they would allow it to be included in the book. He also wanted to know whether the place was truly as haunted as its reputation would suggest.

Their answer was a very simple one: *It most definitely is; come along and see for yourself.*

And so he did.

Owners Kimm and Cami Andersen, along with their partner Dusty Kingston, arranged for Richard and his colleagues to be escorted on a guided tour of the hospital. They duly spent the next couple of hours poking into every dark and dusty nook and cranny, learning about the huge cast of ghosts that haunted its many rooms and hallways.

Kimm ushered the visitors toward a row of plastic chairs in what was usually the main entrance hall; it was off-season, and so the Asylum would not open up as a haunt for several more months, which made it the ideal venue for a little show-and-tell.

Through the course of the next half-hour, Kimm walked the Colorado team through the wide variety of bizarre and unusual media that had been accumulated in the Asylum 49 archives during the past decade. The paranormal nature of some of this material was open to interpretation, but the investigators were impressed with the Andersens' willingness to try and debunk or explain anything for which a rational solution could be found.

A case in point: Visitors had captured what appeared to be two rows of illuminated words or lettering shining on one of the walls in the Nursery. Puzzled and more than a little excited, Kimm and his colleagues located the exact spot of wall on which the luminous writing had appeared, next to the window and behind one of the cribs. Nothing seemed to be amiss in the room, and so they began to experiment with a little flash photography, shooting pictures from different positions and angles from all around the room. When the results were carefully examined, the Asylum 49 staff noticed something very interesting. Several of their own photographs *also* contained an almost identical set of writing, and once again it appeared to be projected onto the wall.

After much scrutiny and searching the room from top to bottom, the source of the mysterious writing was uncovered: It turned out to be the metal fittings for the oxygen cylinders, which were catching the light from the flash and reflecting it back across the room onto the wall, where it was duly captured by the camera lens. The photograph is now used as a cautionary tale for guest investigators at Asylum 49, a reminder that there is often a perfectly rational explanation for what might at first glance seem to be paranormal.

The small crew from the Boulder County Paranormal Research Society (BCPRS) were impressed with Kimm's willingness to throw out some examples of what, in the hands of those with less integrity, would have been presented as evidence of the paranormal. "If in doubt, throw it out!" is a healthy approach to take when evaluating such claims, and so a number of photos of "orbs" (which were almost certainly dust particles) were discarded right off the bat. Long, thin strips of light that stretched across the image and out of the frame were easily explained away as being strands of the photographer's own hair, for example, or insects passing through the frame.

Once the discards had been dealt with, a solid body of other photographic evidence still remained—evidence that could not be explained away and discounted quite so easily.

One of the photos was taken during a paranormal investigation, and shows a male investigator clad in shorts, a T-shirt, and a baseball cap, standing in front of an x-ray machine; he is looking off toward the left side of the frame, and a fellow investigator simply took a shot of him for reference purposes—nothing unusual was noted at the time that the photograph was taken, and there were no other people present apart from the photographer and the investigator himself.

Although the overhead lights were turned off at the time and the room was very shadowy, there was more than enough ambient light for the camera to record the appearance of an uninvited extra guest in this photograph. At the extreme left border of the image stands a thin sliver of what looks like a male figure, wearing some sort of lab coat with a collar and a high breast pocket.

What's maddeningly frustrating about this particular photograph is the fact that, if the photographer had only just been pointing the camera

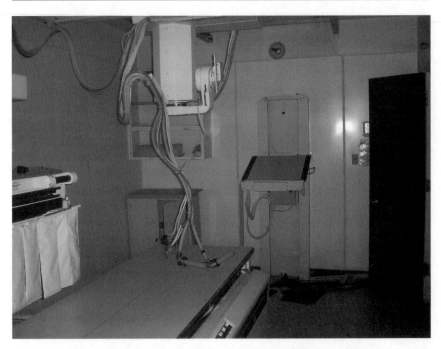

Photo of the x-ray room with equipment that was left behind.

a *fraction* of an inch to the left, we might well be staring at the image of a full-bodied apparition. Of course, one could just as easily look at it from the opposite point of view: If the camera lens had been pointing any further to the right, or taken just an instant later, then it may well not have captured anything at all.

Is this perhaps the shadowy apparition of a former doctor, still making his rounds all these years later? If even a handful of the stories surrounding the old Tooele Valley Hospital are true, then that is entirely possible. But the opinion held by the Asylum 49 team is that the figure in the photograph is that of an x-ray technician named Peter, who had once worked at the hospital, and seems to have enjoyed the experience so much that he has returned to visit after his death.

"What makes you think it's Peter?" Richard wanted to know. "Is it because the equipment in the room behind him is used for taking x-rays?"

"Partly," Kimm answered, "but there's more to it than that. Peter's very active around the Asylum. He turns up on EVPs quite often."

"Can we listen to one?" Jason asked. Kimm nodded, and with a few quick mouse-clicks brought up a hissing audio file through the speakers.

"Tell us your name," asked the voice of a female investigator. Heartbeats later, a soft male voice whispered an answer: *Peter Hansford.*

"Wow," Sean said, genuinely impressed. "What else have you got?"

As it turned out, Kimm had plenty more. The next slide was a photograph of the main hallway. He explained that it had been taken by a friend of his, who had wanted to take his father ghost-hunting while he was visiting Tooele. The Andersens had loaned him a camera and allowed him access to the Asylum overnight, locking the two men inside and wishing them both the very best of luck.

Just as with the previous photograph containing the ghostly x-ray technician, nothing out of the ordinary had been seen at the time that it was taken. The visitor had taken a number of shots in sequence as he walked toward the end of the corridor, observing nothing but an empty corridor both with his own eyes and through the viewfinder.

One can easily imagine their surprise when, on scrolling through the downloaded images the following day, the figure of a large man could be seen at the distant end of the corridor. He was standing directly in front of the wooden double doors that lead into the main entrance hall, the one in which the slideshow was currently being given for the benefit of the investigators from Colorado. He appears to have his hands in his pockets, and seems very nonchalant and unselfconscious about being photographed.

By far the most disturbing thing about the man, however, is his face. When the image is enlarged on a computer monitor, his face looks a lot like the face of a circus character, with cartoonish, caricature-like upsweeping eyebrows and a grin that would not look out of place on the face of a clown.

"I'd like to introduce you to Jeremy," Kimm began. He went on to tell the investigators about the spirit of a man who was hideously burned in a fire during his lifetime, and went on to become a patient at the Tooele Valley Hospital. Kimm had unwittingly offended Jeremy by saying out loud that he looked like a member of the hip-hop duo Insane Clown Posse; Kimm hadn't been aware of Jeremy's horrific injuries at the time, and didn't know that he wore a burn mask to cover his facial disfigurement.

Jeremy's full-body apparition didn't appear in any of the photographs taken either before or after that one single frame. It was almost as though he had chosen to put in an appearance just once, to make the visitors aware of his presence, and then disappeared again, his point made. A smoky, burning smell always accompanies Jeremy's manifestations; we will return to his story later in this book.

Of the several child ghosts who haunt the hospital, perhaps the least camera-shy is a young boy named Thomas. An image of his tiny shadowy form peeping around the edge of a doorframe was followed by what the Asylum 49 team believes to be his face, appearing at adult chest height in a different open doorway.

Other fascinating photographs had been taken in the mirror maze, a twisting labyrinth of dead ends and switchbacks in which all of the walls are covered with reflective glass. The maze is well-known amongst Asylum 49 staff as a hotbed of paranormal activity, and indeed many of the people who work at the haunt—particularly the females—regard it as the dark heart of the entire place, which seems to attract the most negative and malevolent energies.

More than one visitor to the Asylum has wandered through the mirror maze, pausing every once in a while to take flash photographs in the gloom. Sometimes, all that appears is the reflection of the photographer themselves, their head and shoulders usually drowned out by the glare of the flash; but on other occasions, something more remarkable takes place. When the photographs are reviewed afterward, ghostly extras appear, in the form of either isolated faces or, if conditions are right, human figures.

It is a commonly held belief among members of the paranormal community that electronic voice phenomena (EVPs) are the voices of the dead, manipulating some as-yet unknown properties of sound in an attempt to make their presence known to the living. Since some of the earliest EVP voices were documented by pioneers Konstantin Raudive and Friedrich Jurgenson back in the 1960s, a fierce debate has raged concerning the nature of these "voices from beyond"—are they truly discarnate spirits, whether of deceased human beings or extradimensional entities, or simply patterns in the static, stray radio transmissions, or some other form of natural phenomena that we don't entirely understand yet? Are we simply hearing what we want to hear?

Suffice it to say that the jury is still out, and is likely to remain so for the foreseeable future. What *can* be said with certainty is that a number of truly impressive examples of electronic voice phenomena have been captured within the walls of the old Tooele Valley Hospital, not only by those who own and work there, but also by visitors. Many different models of voice recorders have been used to capture them.

Kimm began to play a selection of his favorite EVPs for Richard, Sean, and Jason, who all listened attentively with their eyes closed.

I'm goin' with you! said one voice, which sounded rather menacing. Kimm explained that although the Asylum 49 tour guides always advised visitors to tell any spirits that they must remain inside the building when the visitor went home, the ghosts didn't always obey the rules in that respect.

You'll be mine! was an equally sinister one, whispered in a male voice with a definite undertone of menace.

You're dead . . . two words full of malevolance, and an EVP that sent a chill down the spine of even the most experienced investigators in the room. Death and dying are a common theme amongst the recordings captured at Asylum 49, something not entirely unexpected for a hospital. *I'm dying,* says another male voice in an eerily matter-of-fact manner.

We died here, said the first voice in what would turn out to be a two-part EVP. *Caught a bullet* came immediately afterward. Had the investigators perhaps recorded the voices of patients who had been shot dead and subsequently died in the Emergency Room?

"So can you feel it coming towards you?" asks a female investigator of her colleagues on still another recording, "or do you just feel it right when they are there?" Just a second later, the sound of a childish voice whispers: *I'm here now.* (The *now* is delivered in an uber-creepy way, and can only be intended to be as frightening and intimidating as possible.)

Not all of the EVPs were of such a disturbing nature, however. As we have said before, the ghosts of several children are believed to haunt the former hospital premises. The voice of one young girl is very clearly heard calling *Mom!* on an EVP, while the investigators who are speaking in the foreground are sadly oblivious.

The exact spot in which the ghost of a little girl may have appeared
to one of the authors.

"Is that who you want to touch?" asks an investigator during an EVP session, presumably indicating one of her companions. *Yeah,* comes the distinctly surly response.

On another audio clip, a male investigator asks any spirit present to please speak loudly for him. In response, the sound of a child singing a wordless tune can be heard in the background. The song concludes with a playful giggle from the unseen singer.

An EVP that definitely tugs at the heartstrings contains the voice of a young boy, who sounds as if he is cold and upset. *Don't touch my blanket!* the boy cries. He pronounces the word "blanket" as "bwanket," which is entirely fitting with his young age. The Asylum 49 team believes this to be the voice of Christian, who we will meet again in later chapters.

With the presentation finished, the Andersens led the small team of investigators on a guided tour of the hospital. As the small group went through each room, their hosts detailed the list of paranormal activity that had been reported there, and then left the tired but enthusiastic trio to their work. Locking the exterior doors behind as he headed home for the night, Kimm left them with a cheery "Good night—and good luck!"

That first night at Asylum 49 turned out to be a complete bust. Nothing happened of note, and things were so quiet that by the time four o'clock rolled around, the three investigators were beginning to drift off to sleep in the far too comfortable chairs inside the chapel. After one last dawn walk-through of the old hospital, the boys from Colorado collected up their equipment and headed back to their respective motel rooms in order to catch a few hours of sleep before their long drive back.

The evidence review also turned out to be completely negative: There were no EVPs or anomalies to be found on the various recordings that had been made. Nonetheless, Richard felt that there was still a lot more to the old Tooele Valley Hospital than met the eye. When he contacted the Andersens again, Kimm and Cami were just as disappointed as he was.

"I think I know why you didn't catch anything," Cami told Richard a few days later. "You guys were here off-season. The haunt isn't up and running—we're just renovating and building new stuff for Halloween this year. Yeah, there are a few paranormal groups coming through and investigating, but most of the time there are no more than two or three people in there."

"That's not a whole lot of energy to fuel paranormal activity," Richard mused, thinking it over.

"You guys should come back when the energy's at its highest," she replied confidently. "You know we get well over 30,000 people through here every Halloween season?"

"That's a *lot* of energy."

"Right . . . and it's a lot of potential observers too. It's no coincidence that October and November are when the ghosts are most active."

That made total sense to Richard. "When's your busiest night?"

Cami laughed. "Halloween, of course! We're packed to the rafters on Halloween night. This place goes *crazy*."

Just as the lady had said, Halloween . . . of course! The more he thought about it, the more that Richard came to think that she was right. Asylum 49 would be full of people for hours on end, from early evening until the stroke of midnight and beyond; and not just any people either, because these would be *scared* people, if the actors who were working the haunt were doing their jobs properly. Emotions would be running high, with frights, chills, and scares aplenty going on throughout the entire building.

What better night for the *real* ghosts of the hospital to come out and show themselves?

"I'll do it," Richard decided on the spot, "but it has to be more than just one night. Let's make it a working week—shall we say five or six days?"

"Deal."

x x x x x

October 31st happened to fall on a Saturday night in 2015. It was still dark when Richard and Sean started out on the long drive west to Tooele. Apart from carrying a week's worth of clothing each and a small mountain of scientific equipment that would be used during the course of their investigation, the pickup truck was hauling a few extra surprises.

One was a very expensive mannequin, the same sort that is commonly used to train EMTs, paramedics, and nurses at healthcare institutions all around the world. The mannequin had a realistic airway (into which breathing tubes could be inserted through the mouth) and lungs that would inflate when ventilated with a bag-valve mask. Rubber tubes ran through his one arm, into which needles could be poked and drugs injected. He could even be defibrillated for real, thanks to a pair of electrodes implanted inside the chest wall; it would turn out to be a very useful feature, because Richard was also bringing with him a state-of-the-art cardiac monitor. When it was hooked up to a patient (whether real or simulated), this piece of cutting-edge medical technology could speed up a patient's heart rate if it was too slow, or shock it with up to 360 joules of electricity if it was racing too fast.

The paramedic chief was also bringing a complete airway management kit and a set of expired drugs along with him, not to mention an IV tubing hookup and range of needles and catheters through which to administer them. That was a lot of equipment, taking up a sizeable portion of the flatbed of Richard's truck, but he hoped that it would be well worth the bother because he had a very special purpose in mind for them: an experiment which, to his knowledge, had never been performed by paranormal investigators before.

Arriving in Tooele in the early afternoon, the boys stowed their personal gear in their hotel room (which backed directly onto the local cemetery) and then drove to Asylum 49 to meet up with the rest of the Boulder County Paranormal Research Society investigators. Some had flown in, whereas others had driven; some would be there for the full course of the investigation—five nights—and others could only stay for a few days, but all were full of eager anticipation for the exciting case that lay ahead of them.

It was to be an investigation that none of them would ever forget.

The roll call of investigators was filled by a diverse and motley cast of characters, each of whom brought a different set of skills and life experiences to the investigation of Asylum 49.

A paranormal investigator for 20 years in both the United Kingdom and the United States, Richard was a chief paramedic and volunteer firefighter. Along with his wife Laura, he had founded the Boulder County Paranormal Research Society in 2006, and currently served as its director.

Sean worked as a detailer for an auto company. He was a stocky guy, built like a fireplug, with a great sense of humor and a work ethic to match. Sean was the guy who would get the job done to the best of his ability, no matter how tough it was or what it was that you were asking of him. He was the team's workhorse, and always had a joke or quip on hand to lighten the mood.

Jason Fellon also worked in the medical field, as a pharmacy technician. Along with his wife Linda, who had remained in Colorado, Jason was the team's resident gearhead. Between them, the Fellons had amassed an arsenal of equipment for use in researching the paranormal, one that cost almost as much as a new car—rather appropriate when one considered the bumper sticker on the back of their own car that read "I'd rather be ghost hunt-ing." Analytical and intensely motivated, Jason was itching to return to the Asylum at the height of its activity and start to uncover its secrets.

Catlyn was the team's resident academic, holding a theology-based doc-torate and teaching religious studies, philosophy, and women's studies at a community college. She was more than capable of approaching a situation from either a faith-based or scientific perspective, not to mention perform-ing non-denominational blessing ceremonies when circumstances required it. Catlyn had also brought her husband Greg along with her for the ride, on what was to be his first ever paranormal investigation. Richard believed that having a first-timer along for the ride offered a valuable change in perspec-tive, because guests like Greg weren't subject to the same prejudices toward the paranormal as the more seasoned investigators were. They could often serve as a much-needed breath of fresh air during a case. It also didn't hurt in the least that Greg was highly skilled in the arts of audio analysis, and had become the team's go-to guy for judgment calls on the various EVPs that they captured.

Nor was Greg the only first-timer. For years, Richard had been bugged by his boss, Jennifer, for the opportunity to accompany BCPRS on an inves-tigation. Jennifer (Jen to her friends) was a chief paramedic of many years' standing, and having a fellow paramedic on hand would be a critical part of the medically based experiment that he was planning; he had therefore extended an invitation to Jen, who had made the drive out to Tooele in the company of her teenage daughter, Autumn. Autumn would act as an extra set of eyes and ears inside the hospital, while serving as a trainee investigator for the duration of the case.

When investigating a location with as much square footage as the for-mer Tooele Valley Hospital, it would be almost impossible to bring too many pairs of skilled hands along. It was therefore with real gratitude that Richard welcomed two investigators from The Other Side Investigations, a neigh-boring research team that had worked alongside BCPRS for many years. Randy was an experienced I.T. engineer for a major computer hardware man-ufacturer, and his wife Robbin was a Registered Nurse, which once again dovetailed neatly with the planned experiment. Both were paranormal inves-tigators of many years' standing, not to mention trusted friends, and Robbin had on occasion demonstrated the ability of gathering information via psychic means. That, too, was something that would be put to the test during the investigation of Asylum 49.

It was no coincidence that Richard and his team had chosen October 31st as their first night to conduct an investigation. According to projections, the Asylum was expected to see record numbers of visitors, each one of them a potential energy source for the spirits to manipulate as they saw fit. The Colorado-based team would have the luxury of investigating the place on its busiest night of the year, and then it would be closed for the rest of the week, giving them a quieter, more controllable environment with which to work.

But first there was one small matter to get out of the way. Sensing a once-in-a-lifetime opportunity, Richard and some of his teammates really wanted to get their hands dirty in the most entertaining way possible: They wanted to work in the haunted house on Halloween night.

The owners didn't take much convincing. Although the visitors had made a half-hearted effort to justify investigating the building while it was actually operating as a haunted house attraction, the truth was that they simply wanted to *play;* after all, how often does one get the chance to wear a bucket-load of blood and walk the halls of a haunted hospital, with nothing better to do than terrify members of the public? For some of them, it really was a dream come true!

Taking a cue from one of his real-world professions, Richard brought a set of threadbare old yellow bunker gear and a firefighting helmet. Along with some carefully applied makeup and blood splatter, it didn't take long for the skillful artists in Asylum 49's workshop to transform him into a zombie firefighter, whose assigned task was to shamble menacingly around the outer grounds of the hospital and photobomb as many of the customers' selfies as he could manage.

Jen and Autumn each donned a set of medical scrubs and became the nursing assistants from hell, and when the evening kicked off at sunset, both would find themselves assisting the demonic nurses that worked the main entrance line, singling out the biggest and baddest-looking customers and pulling them out of line early in order for them to receive the "special attention" of the Asylum doctors, which might mean anything from solitary confinement in a cramped, darkened little room, to being sent on ahead through the haunt alone, hounded at every step by the actors who were positioned at key points throughout.

Asylum 49 truly came alive when darkness fell, and a huge line of eager customers was soon snaking around the parking lot and out onto the sidewalk. Eerie but jaunty music pumped out from speakers, and there was a carnival atmosphere among those who were waiting to buy a ticket, before signing the obligatory waiver that comes as part of the price of admission for a full-contact haunt. Customers sealed the deal with a thumbprint before being allowed past the entry point, and some wondered whether they would indeed be truly safe inside the foreboding walls of the old hospital that now awaited them.

With Richard, Jen, and Autumn really getting into the spirit of their new roles, the rest of the team congregated in the security room, watching the progress of the shrieking customers on the banks of CCTV monitors. Cameras were positioned at key points throughout the haunt, intended to ensure the safety of both the customers and the staff. The investigators laughed as, time after time, visitors would turn a corner and be caught in the clutches of some extremely creepy performers, which included evil-looking nuns and priests, doctors (accompanied by sinister nurses and nursing assistants), clowns, werewolves, and vampires. The soundtrack was a mix of unnerving noises, with the softly spoken dialogue of the performers competing with high-pitched screams, the mechanical roar of a chainsaw, or the growl of a monster getting ready to pounce.

The night soon took a sad turn when Jason, who was in the process of setting up for the coming investigation, received some frightening news from home: His son had experienced a sudden medical emergency and needed immediate surgery. Family naturally took precedence over all else, and Jason immediately packed away his equipment and arranged to take the first flight back to Denver. The team was sorry to see him go, but completely understood his reasons and supported his decision (his son would go on to make a full recovery).

As the night wore on, everybody could feel the atmosphere starting to build. It wasn't exactly *eerie* per se, but there was an almost indefinable *something* in the air within those haunted hallways. Certainly, more than one customer had gotten seriously freaked out: In one memorable case, a man dressed as a giant banana lost control of his bodily functions when he encountered one of the more disturbing performers. Following long-held Asylum 49 tradition, when a customer soiled themselves, Kimm awarded the actor in question an on-the-spot $50 cash prize!

The doors were due to be shut at midnight. With the witching hour just a little more than an hour away, Richard decided that he would like to experience the haunt for himself, from a customer's point of view. Getting permission from Kimm, Cami, and Dusty, he quickly doffed the firefighter helmet and jacket and made his way to the front of the building, with the express intention of experiencing Asylum 49 in a whole new way.

Despite the fact that he had been behind the scenes during the daylight hours, navigating the maze of scares and surprises still proved to be an experience that set Richard's heart racing. After about 45 minutes, he found himself in one of the darkened corridors close to the chapel. A grotesque figure wearing denim dungarees was sitting in a recliner. Before Richard had a chance to react, the figure raised what looked like a shotgun and pulled the trigger. Although the gun fired only compressed air, the bang was deafeningly loud in such an enclosed space, and Richard felt as though he was close to having a heart attack because of the sudden shock.

Still recovering from the intensity of the unexpected scare, he didn't pay much attention to the little girl and what he assumed was her mother at first. They were entering the shotgun room just as he was leaving, but the Asylum 49 performer didn't seem to react to their presence, and certainly didn't fire the fake weapon again. The girl was young, somewhere between seven and ten years of age by Richard's estimation, and dressed in a period-era white lace dress, with long, flowing locks of dark hair running down past her shoulders. She was tugging on the shirt of a lady who was dressed in contemporary clothing, playfully dragging the older woman into the room despite what seemed to be some feigned reluctance on her part.

Thinking nothing of it, Richard finished out his journey through the haunt and made his way back to the security center, where Kimm and Cami Andersen were hunkered down in front of the CCTV monitors, along with the rest of the BCPRS investigators.

"Have fun?" Cami grinned. "I loved the part where you nearly karate-chopped the actor in the hallway!"

"Couldn't help it." Richard ran a hand through sweat-soaked hair, only now realizing just how nerve-wracking an experience the last hour had been. "The ophthalmologist was super creepy. So was the little girl in the white lacy dress."

"Pieces (nicknamed PJ) is the name of the guy that plays the eye doc," said Kimm distractedly, still scanning the camera feeds as he talked. "He invented that character and he's really put *a lot* of work into developing it." Almost as an aside, he added, "We don't have anybody playing a girl in a white lacy dress though."

"You don't? That's weird, because I definitely saw her. She was pulling some lady along by the front of her shirt, pulling her into the room with the guy in the rocking chair."

"Describe her," Cami instructed. Richard did, and the Andersens shot one another a knowing look. "There's one younger girl who works here named Lexi, but she wasn't in that particular room at all tonight. I think that you saw our little Sara."

"Sara?" Richard asked, confused.

"One of the ghosts here," Kimm explained. "She likes to wander around the place, and you just pretty much described her perfectly."

"I'm not sure about that. She was as solid as you are." Even as the words were coming out of his mouth, Richard was aware of how stupid they were. Many apparitions were described as being completely solid, and were often mistaken for living people. It was starting to dawn on him that he might just have encountered one of Asylum 49's resident spirits and it had never even crossed his mind to take a picture, despite having a phone in his pocket all along.

"You said there was a younger girl that's working here tonight," Sean pointed out. Cami nodded and looked up at the clock, which was now reading a quarter past midnight.

"Lexi. Look, we're still shutting down and none of the actors will have gone home yet. They'll all be hanging out in the Cast Room. Let's go and see if the girl you saw is in there."

The Cast Room was where the performers got to unwind after a busy night's work. It had its own little kitchen area, restrooms, and couches to relax on. The atmosphere was warm and friendly when Cami and Richard walked in, full of happy people chatting to one another about the night's events. The fact that at least half of them looked like murder victims—and the other half looked like their murderers—somehow didn't detract from the family atmosphere in the slightest.

Apologizing for stepping on the occasional set of toes, Richard walked from chair to chair, looking at each performer's face and costume carefully. The dark-haired child in the white lace dress was nowhere to be found. Cami was kind enough not to say "I told you so," but he was no less troubled for that. It was beginning to look as though one of Asylum 49's ghosts had put in an appearance that night, right in front of a seasoned paranormal investigator, and he hadn't even recognized it until long after the fact.

"Don't worry about it too much," Cami said as they made their way back to the security center. "You might have missed out on this one, but you've got the rest of the week ahead of you. Who knows what will happen when it's just you guys alone in the building?"

Richard nodded thoughtfully. Cami was right. A lot could happen during the space of the next few days. Gathering his team together, he started to tell them about the incident with the little girl.

It was time to go to work.

3

The Main Hallway

If Asylum 49 has a backbone, then it must surely be the main hallway. Running from one end of the hospital to the other, all of the rooms and wings extend from this hallway like peripheral nerves branching off the spinal cord.

The long corridor carpeted in green with fluorescent lights above is typical of any hospital, and runs the length of the building, connecting the ER on the south side to the maternity wing on the north side. Wooden doors with gold foil lettering on them that indicate which room is which, break up the hall's half wood-paneled, half whitewashed walls. The hallway is made up of professional rooms from staff lounges and locker rooms to the extremely haunted conference room. Large double doors, situated almost at the center of the main hall, open up to the west into yet another hall, where the kitchen and laundry room area once was, but has since been converted into the cast rooms, makeup room, and costume room.

What was once full of the hustle and bustle of medical staff is now still and empty, but when the lights go out, shadowy figures silently roam the darkness and lurk in the doorways, beckoning paranormal investigators to seek them out and tell their story.

It is also one of the most paranormally active areas of the entire building, and so it seems only fitting that we begin our journey into the heart of Asylum 49 right there.

Resident psychic Misty Grimstead has no shortage of ghostly incidents to recount regarding the main hallway. It is one of her favorite locations in which to sit and "hall-gaze," as she likes to call the practice of turning out the lights, sitting still, and waiting for the Asylum's long-dead inhabitants to appear, like woodland creatures tentatively emerging into the open air after a long winter in hibernation.

Some of these phantoms fit the profile for intelligent entities—they will sometimes interact with the living, going so far as to answer questions put to them in the form of EVPs. Others seem more residual, being the images and sounds of those who once walked these halls, either as patients or members of staff; their presence is played back in some way that we do not yet understand.

One such residual ghost is that of a nurse who Misty happened to encounter one day, going about the commonplace business of pushing a patient in a wheelchair between rooms. Neither nurse nor patient seemed aware of Misty's existence, and such apparitions are usually no more interactive than the images on a TV screen.

Perhaps the most intriguing of the main hallway's entities is a spirit named Robert. He is known to show himself in shadow form. He's tall and broad and has been seen with a cane walking across the main hallway, peering inside the conference room doors. Robert is also known to have a unique sense of humor, and will often be heard cracking jokes during EVP sessions. He has been spotted sneaking into the conference room, trying to remain unseen by belly-crawling like a soldier under fire, or by jumping out at passers-by, giving them one heck of a startle.

He will also make an appearance when least expected. During a rather busy night at the haunted house attraction, Cami and Kimm Andersen were at the front entrance, hidden behind a curtain that was stretched across the hall; they were directing the flow and size of groups coming through the haunt. Cami suddenly felt that she was being watched and turned around. Standing against the wooden doors behind them, she saw a tall shadow. It didn't take long for her to recognize it as Robert.

Photo of the maternity hall on the left and main hall on the right.

She turned to Kimm and said, "Look who's behind us. Can you see him?"

"Oh, it's Robert," Kimm replied.

Robert stood there watching the couple for quite some time and didn't seem to be leaving any time soon.

"I'm going to go get the Sony Night-Shot camcorder and hopefully catch him on video," Kimm said.

Kimm left, and Cami continued to direct the haunted house traffic while watching Robert, hoping he was still there when Kimm got back with the camcorder.

As luck would have it, Robert was content to stay and watch as Kimm set up the camcorder facing the double doors where he stood and pressed record.

Kimm looked at Robert, and noticed that in the dimly lit hall he could be misconstrued as the shadowy area of the corner and decided to see if he could get some movement out of Robert. "We can see you, Robert, you're kinda freaking Cami out. Can you move to another area of the hall please?"

Without skipping a beat, the large shadow walked across the hall to the other side of the door.

Kimm laughed and told Robert that they could still see him and that he looked like a child with his nose in the corner, but he stayed right where he was.

They went back to working the haunted house traffic and left the camcorder recording, but each time they walked over to check on the camera it had been turned off. Knowing for certain that the camcorder had a full charge and had been working flawlessly until now, they couldn't figure out why it had suddenly begun to turn itself off. Perhaps Robert was toying with them (or perhaps not), but that still didn't explain why it had captured no footage of the shadow, which had been clear for them to see on the camcorder screen at the time, when they later reviewed the snippets of recording that they had been able to get.

Robert is also decidedly picky about whom he chooses to spend time and communicate with, and really isn't shy about making it known if he doesn't like someone.

Grainy video footage of a shadowy figure that Asylum 49 staff members believe to be Robert was captured during a ghost tour, when he tacked himself on to the back of a group of visitors. None of them noticed the uninvited extra guest who followed along silently in their wake, taking in every word and watching all that they did.

It is Misty's belief that Robert is a kind-hearted soul, who has taken it upon himself to guard the children who are known to haunt the chapel.

A more sinister spirit by far is Jeremy, who haunts the same stretch of hallway—though he has been known to roam about the hospital at will, when the mood takes him.

Severely burned in a fire, Jeremy's apparition has melted and distorted facial features that are consistent with third-degree burns. Jeremy is reputed to be, in the words of some female members of staff, "quite a pervert," and has followed Misty home on more than one occasion. He took great delight in peeping in at her while she was showering.

One thing that Jeremy is *not*, however, is camera-shy. A visitor once snapped a photograph of Jeremy standing at the midpoint of the hallway, and it appeared at first that he was wearing a clown mask—in fact, so much so that Kimm Andersen jokingly referred to him as "the clown-faced guy" and less charitably, the "insane clown posse."

It took the intervention of Misty in her capacity as a psychic medium to inform Kimm that he was really hurting Jeremy's feelings, because what he had taken to be burn makeup was actually horribly disfiguring burn trauma.

"It was my first week working here, and when I was sleeping in bed one night, I had a dream that I was standing right here in the middle of the main hallway, talking to a spirit," she recalls. "The spirit kept telling me: 'I don't like Kimm.' When I asked why, he told me that he died in a fire and that was how his face looked now. He didn't like Kimm mocking his appearance."

When Misty explained the reason behind Jeremy's unusual appearance to Kimm, he immediately stopped referring to him as a clown; however, Jeremy seems to be something of the grudge-bearing type, and hasn't quite forgiven Kimm yet—he still harbors considerable resentment toward him.

Other photos show Jeremy as an extremely tall, well-built, and intimidating shadow figure, usually standing in the same area. He is something of a voyeur, and likes to watch the living without making them aware of his presence.

Jeremy is also well-known for his propensity to lie, preferring to misrepresent himself as Robert, or any of the Asylum's other spirit personalities when it suits his purpose. *Why* he feels the need to masquerade as somebody else isn't quite clear. Misty's take on Jeremy is that he has very low self-esteem, and craves nothing more than a little attention from visitors—particularly female ones.

He is never able to conceal the stench of smoke, however, which seems to accompany him everywhere he goes; for those paranormal investigators who are well-versed in the history of the Asylum, the smell of burning is a real give-away that they are communicating with Jeremy, no matter *what* name the spirit has given or type of voice turns up on their EVPs.

When not lurking in the main hallway, Jeremy can also be found haunting the former staff lounge and kitchen nearby.

Asylum 49 security guard, Robert "Buck" Helige, Jr., once had his own close encounter with the spirit of Jeremy. He, his young son, and his brother were busily engaged in stringing lengths of cable for the in-house CCTV system, which would need to be in prime condition before the fast-approaching Halloween season.

Buck and his brother were working on the upper rungs of a ladder in the main hallway, just outside the lobby doors and the old nurses' station. Their task was to carefully site a camera to cover the corridor, run a cable up to it, and then mount it securely high up on the wall. Buck's son was footing the ladder, making sure that it didn't swing out from under the two men, and occasionally handing them tools.

Suddenly, the double doors that led to the main lobby opened, and a man walked out into the hallway. Buck noticed that he was wearing some sort of bandaging around his face and neck, although a pair of gleaming eyes and a mouth were visible through gaps.

The man turned and looked at them for a moment, as though trying to work out exactly what it was that they were doing. For their part, the three men simply froze, watching wordlessly as the stranger walked along the length of the main hallway to its far end, before disappearing entirely from sight.

Sensing that something wasn't quite right where the interloper was concerned, Buck's brother turned to him and asked Buck if he had just seen the same thing that he had. Buck was silent for a moment, having a pretty good idea of who it was that had just walked in, but also not wanting to frighten his young son.

Before he could answer, Buck's son asked whether they had both just seen the man who had just walked in—and also, hadn't they all been able to smell the smoke?

4

From the Cradle to the Grave

All three of the nursery rooms (the neonatal intensive care unit, or NICU, the Special Nursery, and the plain nursery itself) are directly connected with one another, and are usually unlit and shadowy, with blinds permanently drawn on the windows to the outside world and to the main hallway.

The walls are covered with posters displaying the intricacies of human anatomy in all its glory. In stark contrast, the patient beds are home to nightmarish caricatures of the human body, in the form of mannequins whose torsos have been sewn together by one of the demented surgeons that prowls the haunted house attraction, assisted by ghoulish nurses wielding saws, scalpels, and an array of terrifying tools. Every surface is splattered with arterial blood spray, which has also reddened the modesty screens and other pieces of medical equipment such as the metal IV poles that seem to be everywhere.

The "Special Nursery" was the name for that part of the hospital that was intended for children in need of that little bit of extra attention from the doctors and nurses of the day, those with special needs in today's parlance. It is located along the main hallway on the south side, and faces patient rooms One and Two.

In order to enter it, one has to go through a small anteroom, which was used as both a lab and for the performance of such relatively routine procedures as circumcision. Today, the room houses a three-person human centipede, much to the delight and disgust of those visitors who chance upon it in the dark.

When watching the security monitors during a live run-through of the haunted house attraction, one vigilant staff member saw the apparition of a little girl walking through this anteroom and into the Special Nursery. No young children were acting as part of the performance in that section of the hospital, and it is intriguing to note that the little girl did not appear on any of the cameras that covered the adjoining rooms or hallway, which makes the obvious explanation—that of her being a flesh and blood child—difficult to believe; were she the child of a customer, Asylum 49 staff would not have separated her from her parents at such a young age.

The ghosts of both a doctor and a nurse are very active in this section of the building: He is named Nicholas, and the name of the nurse is not yet known. According to resident Asylum 49 psychic Misty Grimstead, although both of these spirits are intelligent rather than residual, neither of them seems to be aware that they are dead: They simply labor on in the belief that they are still at work, and that it is business as usual, going about their duties and caring for patients as they would have done when they were still alive.

"They get mad at me sometimes when I come in here and they feel that I'm getting in their way," she explains, "so I just step aside and let them get on with it."

In order to add to the general confusion and mayhem of the haunt, a volunteer actor who is playing the role of a demonic doctor is stationed in the NICU and Special Nursery during the haunt. With the help of an assistant or two, he tends to target the bigger, cockier customers and singles them out for "special treatment" on his blood-splattered bed. Watching the security camera feed one night at the height of the Asylum's busiest Halloween season so far, Misty was astonished to see a second doctor—presumed to be Nicholas—standing behind the fake horror doctor, who was bending over a somewhat terrified "patient." Nicholas simply hovered, watching all that transpired as the actors delivered their lines and simulated surgery, neither commenting nor interrupting. One can only wonder at his thoughts toward the grim tableaux that was playing out before his eyes.

The Special Nursery has a hidden alcove, which is generally used as a hiding place in which actors can position themselves out of sight, before leaping out on unsuspecting customers. The alcove has its own resident spirit, that of a hearing-impaired patient who doesn't like the hustle and bustle of the haunted house; she tends to appear when things are quieter, and sometimes attempts to communicate via sign language to those lucky few who have caught glimpses of her peeking around the corner of the secret nook.

Residual phenomena also occurs quite frequently throughout the pediatric section of the hospital, including the sound of babies crying, many years after the last infant was born here and placed in one of the nurseries for additional care.

The Nursery itself is haunted by a pair of young children named Sara and Tabitha. They are a pair of playful spirits, who like nothing better than to participate in the haunted house attraction, showing themselves to customers and often hiding under tables and beds, reaching out to snatch at the legs of the unwary as they pass by.

Once Halloween has passed and Asylum 49 closes its doors until the following year, Sara and Tabitha become very sad and melancholy. Sensitives have said that the girls miss the energy and feeling of sheer playfulness and chaos that the haunt brings with it. Sara is said to take it particularly hard when the season is done, and so it is not unknown for members of the Asylum 49 staff to come and spend time in the Nursery once the building is quiet and deserted, simply sitting there and keeping the girls company. Some even buy toys for them to play with.

Sara is a little girl with dark hair who was a patient here. She died of pneumonia. Witnesses have described Sara as being approximately six years old, and wearing a white dress or gown of some kind.

Tabitha wears an old-style yellow dress when she appears, and was also once a patient at the Tooele Valley Hospital. Her cause of death is not known for sure, but based upon a conversation that she had with Tabitha, Misty believes it to have been a brain tumor, or something very similar, such as an intracranial bleed.

Tabitha is the quieter, more introverted of the two girls, whereas Sara is a little on the rambunctious side: One Asylum staff member woke up after dozing off in the Nursery to find Sara playfully licking her hand!

In this area there have also been encounters with doctors and nurses who are carrying on as if it's just another day at the office, and also with some of the patients that they once tended. One noteworthy apparition in this area is that of Bonnie, a lady in her 50s who has short, strawberry-blond hair. Mediums have claimed that Bonnie passed away after being afflicted with cancer.

Those who have seen Bonnie describe her as wearing a hospital gown, and are struck by the fact that she is shuffling around with one hand on an IV stand, which is a tall, wheeled metal pole from which hangs a bag of fluid.

Why an adult cancer patient should choose to haunt a part of the hospital once dedicated to the care of infants and children was a mystery that went unexplained until a sensitive who was trying to communicate with Bonnie was told that Bonnie's purpose in the Nursery is twofold: First, she is searching for her husband, and looks in vain for him throughout the hospital, and secondly, she comes to visit the babies who she thinks are still to be found in there, not wanting to accept that there hasn't been a flesh and blood child cared for in the Nursery for many years now.

Through the course of the last 10 years, a constant stream of visitors have toured and investigated the hospital, including countless sensitives and psychic mediums. Many of them have claimed to see a little girl in the nursery area, and based upon the same description that has been consistently given, it is usually the apparition of Sara that they are seeing, rather than that of the shyer Tabitha. The owners and staff maintained a certain amount of healthy skepticism at first, which gradually diminished when sighting after sighting of the same girl began to mount up, coming in from visitors who were completely unknown to one another, but all telling the same story.

During the Halloween season, the Asylum 49 haunted house attraction is in full swing. Every night, the Andersens and their fellow owners start out by walking through the building, in order to ensure that each actor is in their proper place and is ready to scare. On one particular October night, Kimm Andersen began his inspection at the usual place—the main entrance. He checked the main entry line, which was cordoned off into lanes with the help of strings of IV tubing.

Next, he made his way deeper inside the building, going into the Special Nursery. Bizarrely, nobody was in there, despite a performer having been assigned to that particular room. He walked next door and once again found that it was deserted.

Kimm frowned. Just where the heck *was* everybody? He couldn't help but think that this was how a lot of horror movies started.

Finally reaching the nurses' station that separates the NICU from the regular nursery, he found all of the actors huddled together in the corner.

"What are you guys doing in here?" Kimm wanted to know, exasperated. "It's time to open!"

"We can't work here tonight," one of the actors replied with uncharacteristic nervousness. "Put us on the other side of the hospital if you want, or send us home if you have to, but there's no way we're working in *here!*"

"*Here* meaning this part of the building, not the whole Asylum?" Kimm clarified. The young actor nodded, pale-faced and obviously frightened of *something*. "Why not?"

"Because there's a ghost out in the hallway!" the wide-eyed kid blurted out, looking anxiously past Kimm toward the doorway. "We *saw* her!"

Ghosts in a haunted house, Kimm thought drily, *go figure.* Looking around at what was basically a crowd of scared kids, however, he soon realized that he had a real problem on his hands. Asylum 49 relied on volunteer actors like this to produce the hundreds of scares and chills that kept the customers happy. If they were too scared to do their jobs, that didn't bode well at all. This had to be nipped in the bud, and quickly.

Kimm told the actors to stay put for now while he went to check on the so-called ghost in the hallway. It was probably just the product of their overactive imaginations, the rational, everyday part of his mind reassured him: but another part of his brain, the part that had spent months working inside this haunted building and listening to the paranormal experiences of its visitors, wasn't quite so sure.

He moved aside the heavy black curtain, which shielded the maternity hallway from view, and suddenly stopped dead in his tracks.

There, standing in front of Patient Room Two, was a little girl.

Even to this day, Kimm recalls the scene with total clarity. The little girl was wearing a long white lace night gown, which hung all the way to the floor over her bare feet; long sleeves came down to just above her wrists, and the gown's neckline rose up to the level of her chin. Two tiny hands covered her face, and long black hair flowed down over her shoulders.

Taken aback, Kimm could do little more than look at her in stunned silence as his brain tried to process the fact that he was looking at a full-bodied apparition. If only he had his phone camera with him . . .

It soon occurred to him that not only could he see her, he could also *hear* her. The poor little thing was crying her heart out. At the same time, he was fascinated to discover that the girl's eyes actually glistened with tears. As the father of three children, Kimm's paternal instincts are very finely-tuned—and now they came rushing to the forefront.

"What's wrong, honey?" he asked the ghostly little girl, still not quite believing this was actually happening.

"It's not fair!" she wailed back, struggling to get the words out between sobs. "It's just *not fair*! I want to do what they're doing! I want to *scare* people!"

"That's great for the people who don't work here," Kimm pointed out reasonably, "but the people that *do* work here know that you're not alive—that you are a ghost—and I'm afraid that you're scaring them." He watched her reaction carefully when he pointed out to her that she was dead, knowing that some spirits flatly refuse to believe they may have passed on.

The ghostly little girl didn't argue with him about her incorporeal state; she simply put her hands back in front of her eyes and repeated that it *just wasn't fair!*

Kimm felt genuinely sad for the little girl. All she really wanted was to scare people, probably because she had seen *other* children doing the same thing at the Asylum night after night during the course of the Halloween season. *Is it really so much to ask,* Kimm thought to himself, *that she can lend a hand and feel like she's not being excluded by the other kids?*

He looked around. Hospital beds were staggered at intervals down the length of the maternity hall. On some of the beds lay grotesque mannequins covered by blankets, but the beds at the end of the hall held surprises of an entirely different nature: *They* had live actors concealed in them, primed and ready to jump up and scare the unwary passers-by.

As he looked at the beds, Kimm suddenly had a great idea that he thought might make everyone happy.

"Okay," he said at last, "I'll make you a deal: you *can* scare people, but don't let the other actors *see* you, alright? Go crawl under one of those beds, and then, when people walk by, reach out and grab at their feet."

The little girl's eyes brightened, her tears suddenly replaced with a bright smile, like the sun coming out from behind a cloud to brighten up a dark day.

Kimm wasn't remotely prepared for what happened next. He was half-expecting the ghostly child to scamper off and find a hiding place, but instead, she turned into a nebulous black mist that floated underneath the nearest bed.

Amazed at what he had just seen, Kimm turned and made his way back toward the nurse's station, where the frazzled bunch of actors were nervously anticipating his return. He now understood why they were so frightened, but was absolutely convinced that they weren't in any sort of danger. Composing himself, he took a deep breath and then said, "There's nothing out there. Maybe you're just tired and your eyes are starting to play tricks. It's been a long day already, and you're probably dehydrated. I'll get some sodas for you guys. It's nearly time to open so let's get ready."

The performers seemed less than convinced, so Kimm told them to follow him. Obediently, they trooped out into the now seemingly empty corridor and looked around them. All was silent. Nothing moved. The actors clearly felt much better, and seemed more than a little relieved that there were now no ghosts in the hallway.

"So, are we good?" Kimm asked, taking great care not to look down. The performers nodded, and dispersed to their assigned locations. None of them had any idea what was hiding underneath one of the hospital beds.

With the crisis over, Kimm went through the rest of the haunt and once he was satisfied that nothing else was amiss, opened up the doors for admission. When the horde of eager customers started shuffling forward into the dark bowels of the Asylum, Kimm took some time out to tell some of the volunteers that also worked as tour guides about his interaction with the little girl and moved on to run the haunted house for the night. He wasn't met with nearly as much disbelief as he was expecting, because it turned out that he wasn't the only one to have seen the little girl's ghost.

A short time later, a call came in over the radio asking Kimm to go and talk with the security guards in the maternity hall. He was told that it wasn't an emergency, and so took the time to finish up with a few administrative tasks before making his way to the maternity hallway.

It was getting on to midnight when he finally got there and found a pair of rather nonplussed security guards. Kimm listened without comment as they told him about some ghostly goings-on in the beds in the hallway, which had been reported to them by a pair of Asylum 49 volunteers.

These two female performers had been lying in the beds out there in the corridor, not far from the entrance to the nurseries. Their job had been to jump up and scare the pants off the passers-by. In between their bouts of terrifying the customers, the two girls had watched with horrified fascination as a dark mass floated from bed to bed, before seeming to disappear underneath each one, only to reappear later beneath another one.

The security guards both sounded hesitant. They clearly expected to be ridiculed, but had felt compelled to share the girls' story with somebody. Kimm laughed, and told them about his own encounter with the ghost of the little girl, ending with the way in which she had dissipated into a dark mass and shot beneath one of those very same hospital beds.

For her part, although she trusted her husband's word implicitly, Cami remained somewhat skeptical about Kimm's paranormal encounter.

Her opinion would change dramatically soon enough.

The following year's Halloween season would turn out to be even busier. One night, during the run-up to Halloween, Kimm and Cami were conducting their now-traditional inspection tour prior to opening for business. Working their way from the main hallway, they passed into the Special Nursery, then through into the NICU. Next came the nurses' station, followed by the regular nursery itself.

Everything was just fine, and the Andersens were pleased to see that all of the actors were in position and ready to terrify. Satisfied, the pair walked out into the main hallway near the maternity wing. The hospital beds were staggered along its length, just as they had been on the night when Kimm had encountered the spirit of the little girl. The theme this year, however, was different: the design of the hallway was based on a scene from a film titled *The*

Possession, which concerns a little girl who finds a box at a yard sale—a box that is inhabited by a demon, which subsequently emerges and possesses her.

The scene in question portrays the possessed girl standing beneath an exit light, her head tilted toward the ground with her hair draped over her face. The actress who was playing that same role inside Asylum 49 would say "Daddy . . . *you scared me.*" Then she would laugh, repeating the line as fresh customers came toward her, her voice getting more and more sinister with every repetition.

As the actress was speaking her line, Kimm and Cami watched quietly from the sidelines, hidden in a pool of shadow. Suddenly, Cami heard the voice of a little girl whispering into her ear . . .

"*You scared me.*"

Rather than being frightened, Cami simply laughed. It wasn't the first time that she had experienced a spirit voice whispering into her ear inside the hospital. She told Kimm what she had heard and he wasn't remotely surprised.

"I told you," Kimm grinned in the blackness. "You just met Sara."

Cami needed no further convincing, and spent the rest of the night running around in a state of great excitement. She didn't let a person go by without telling them of her recent experience. When the last customers were close to leaving at the end of the night and the doors were about to be closed and locked behind them, she was still floating on cloud nine. On their way to thank the cast and crew for their hard work that night, she and Kimm made their last rounds of the evening.

The pair walked into the Special Nursery, then into the NICU, and passed through all of the neighboring rooms. As they walked along the hall observing the actors' final performance of the night, Cami noticed an ethereal light illuminating the hall behind them. She turned her head to look behind them, still walking hand in hand with Kimm.

What she saw back there remains with her still.

Silently coming up behind them with outstretched hands was the figure of a little girl in a long, lacy white night gown. Her stringy long black hair hung over a pale gray face in a manner reminiscent of the entity featured in the horror movie *The Grudge*.

Then the silence was broken. As Cami strained her ears to listen, she could hear Sara faintly whispering:

"Daddy . . . you scared me."

x x x x x

Before any formal ghost tour is given at Asylum 49, a multimedia presentation of evidence that has been captured through the years is given, along with stories of paranormal happenings that have been experienced personally by the owners, staff, and visitors. The presentation includes video clips, photographs, and EVP audio files, all of which contain extra elements that are believed to come from the ghostly inhabitants of the former hospital.

Sara is one of the most active and popular ghosts in residence at the Asylum, if we measure it in terms of how frequently her voice shows up on EVP recordings. Late one night during a particular ghost tour, Kimm and Cami were giving their standard presentation to a group of paranormal investigators, who were sitting comfortably on seats inside the main lobby and eagerly anticipating the events of the night ahead.

Standing in front of a large, wall-mounted TV screen, Kimm began to relate the story of his encounter with Sara. Tapping at the computer keyboard, he pulled up a photograph of Sara. Suddenly, a woman sitting in the front row along with her husband suddenly sat bolt upright and gasped. A hand flew up to cover her mouth. The expression on her face was not one of shock, but rather one of recognition.

Cami pointed to the woman and mouthed, "You've seen Sara before, haven't you?" The woman nodded, looking a little flustered, and Cami let her know that she would like to talk with her privately after the presentation.

After the presentation had concluded, the female guest duly approached Cami and Kimm, and began to tell them the story of how she had once encountered Sara's ghost.

During the Halloween season prior to this particular ghost tour, the lady and her husband had gone through the haunted house attraction as customers. When they had made their way through to the section of main hallway outside the nurseries, having dodged more than their fair share of scares along the way, a little girl suddenly appeared out of the darkness. She was wearing a long, lacy white gown and had black hair running down past the middle of her back.

Figuring that it was all part of the show, the female visitor was then surprised when the child grabbed her hand and said she was looking for her mother.

"We'll come with you," she told the child reassuringly, adding that together they would all go and find her mother together. The girl seemed quite happy at their willingness to help, and kept hold of the lady's hand as the trio passed through the main hallway, on into Labor and Delivery, and then outside into that scariest of areas: the clown maze. This mockup of a circus big-top tent has been crafted and partitioned into a cunningly designed labyrinth of twists, turns, and dead ends, scattered amongst which are a variety of creepy Asylum 49 performers. It is not unusual for those who are already frightened of clowns to collapse into a terrified, sobbing mess when venturing into this part of the haunt, and the members of staff keep a watchful eye out for those who need to be discreetly led out via a hidden side exit.

As they negotiated the clown maze, the two customers realized that they had somehow lost the little girl somewhere along the way. With a shrug, they reasoned that the child must have seen her mother and run off to rejoin her.

The couple didn't think about the lost child again until their ghost tour, when they saw the photo of the little girl on the large TV screen hanging on the wall and heard the Andersens tell the backstory of young Sara—for the little girl had told them that Sara was her name.

She still hasn't found her mommy.

x x x x x

During their investigation, Richard, Sean, and Misty had their eyes continually drawn toward the doorway leading from the Nursery out into the main corridor. They all caught flashes of movement, which looked like a head peeping in through the doorway and then back out of sight when it caught the investigators' attention. A strong, cold breeze came through the Nursery during one such sighting, though given the poor insulation of the place, the investigators could not rule out natural drafts as a potential cause.

"I just felt as though my legs were being pulled," Sean said, keeping a wary eye on the doorway. Was Sean experiencing a psychosomatic sensation, brought on because he had been told about the ghostly girls' propensity for swiping at the legs of visitors, or were they genuinely playing with him, reaching out to try and make contact with him?

Given the sheer amount of paranormal activity reported within the vicinity of the three pediatric rooms, the visiting investigators agreed to designate it a probable "hot spot" and to single it out for some dedicated testing.

Late one evening when the other investigators had called it quits for the day, Richard, Sean, and Asylum 49 staff members Tyson and Julie Lemmon made their way over to the Nursery, speaking in the hushed, almost reverential tones that the former hospital seems to inspire in most people. They had made sure to lock up the building first, in order to eliminate the possibility of anybody entering and contaminating their experiments.

"We should try the Human Pendulum," Tyson suggested. "We've gotten some great results using that technique in here."

The Human Pendulum is a controversial technique among paranormal investigators. Some believe that it allows discarnate entities to manipulate the body of the person who volunteers to act as a pendulum, whereas others believe that it can be explained away by involuntary micro-muscular tremors. The volunteer invites the spirits to push him or her in one of four directions in response to questions, thereby giving a "yes" or "no" answer.

Ever eager to get straight into the thick of the action, Sean immediately volunteered to go first. Richard and Julie hung back, recording the experiment on video and audio while Tyson coordinated events.

Standing in a straight but relaxed posture in the center of the Nursery, Sean followed Tyson's coaching, repeating his words out loud into thin air. The other investigators could see him dimly illuminated by the glow of a small flashlight that he held loosely in his right hand: all else in the room was cast in deep shadow.

"Please show me my 'yes,'" Sean began. Nothing happened. He repeated the request a second time.

Slowly but surely, he began to lean toward his right hand side. Richard thought that it was a little spooky to watch.

"Can you please show Sean his 'no'?" Tyson said. Immediately, Sean returned to his center and then began to tilt inexorably over toward his left side now.

"Sean, are you doing that?" Richard asked in disbelief. "You're leaning towards your left."

"No, I ain't doing nothing," Sean answered, every bit as incredulous. "I can't control this thing!"

"You look like you're being pushed. Do you *feel* like you're being pushed?"

Sean said that yes, he did indeed feel that he was being pushed. He likened it to the same sensation as going downhill in a car. Arguably the most down-to-earth, pragmatic member of BCPRS was admitting to feeling an unseen force pushing him gently but firmly off his feet.

Never ones to miss an opportunity to investigate bizarre happenings, Richard and Tyson began to use Sean's "Human Pendulum" as the basis for an impromptu question and answer session. The answers came thick and fast, with Sean being pushed to the right to indicate "yes" and to the left to indicate "no."

"Did you come here tonight with Sean?"

Yes.

"Did you know Sean in a past life?" asked Tyson.

This time, he was pulled backward. When Tyson reminded whatever entities might be present that only yes or no answers were acceptable, Sean was again tugged backward, more sharply this time.

"Okay, show Sean his 'yes' again please." Tyson was attempting to reset the pendulum. Obligingly, Sean was pushed toward the right.

"Are you here to keep Sean safe?"

Yes.

Richard asked a question that, with hindsight, he really wishes he hadn't.

"Are you Sean's grandfather?"

Tyson paused the proceedings as soon as Sean was pushed toward his right. He wasn't comfortable with asking about the specific identity of a spirit during the Human Pendulum experiment, he said, because it allowed those entities who might have less than honorable motives to sometimes masquerade as the loved one of a visitor, and thereby cause them further grief and pain. Sean's grandfather had recently died, and Richard had asked the question reflexively, without thinking through the possible consequences of it—not least of which was how upsetting it might be for Sean, no matter what the answer turned out to be. He still regrets having asked that question to this day.

Sean was understandably a little shaken, and Richard felt like a complete heel. After Sean stepped out into the hallway for a few minutes to take a short break and to gather himself again, the two investigators elected to trade places.

It was interesting to note that for Richard, being pushed forward signified no and being pushed backward indicated yes.

Tyson started out with "Did you come here tonight with Richard?"

Something invisible gently pushed the surprised Englishman backward onto his heels.

Yes.

"Are you always with him?"

Yes.

"Are you from Waverly?" Sean interjected. The two men had investigated at the very haunted Waverly Hills Sanatorium in Louisville, Kentucky, earlier that year, and Richard's voice had been heard speaking by two female investigators down in the underground body chute when he was in fact several stories above them on the roof.

Richard stood still, hardly moving a muscle.

"Did you follow him from Waverly Hills?" Tyson demanded.

Yes.

"Did you follow him to Cripple Creek?" Sean took back the reins, intrigued now. It was a fascinating question. Richard had investigated the old jail at Cripple Creek, Colorado, a few weeks beforehand, and his doppelganger had been seen by another investigator, standing on the balcony and taking photographs: The only problem being that Richard had been secured inside a prison cell at the time, with another investigator standing in the doorway keeping an eye on him. There was no possible way that he could have been in two places at once, or gotten out of the cell to be spotted by the now rather shaken investigator.

No.

"Is there more than one of you following him?"

There was no response, even when the question was repeated several times. The next few questions, whether asked by Sean or Tyson, all went obstinately unanswered. Richard remained standing still. Getting frustrated, they reset Richard's yes and no positions, which both worked the first time.

"Did you know Richard before you passed away?" Tyson asked.

No.

"Okay . . . did you know Richard *after* you passed away?"

Richard rocked backward onto his heels. That was a definite *yes.*

"Did he respond to your accident?" Sean asked, referring to Richard's profession as a paramedic and volunteer firefighter.

No.

"Has Richard seen you before?"

No.

"Do you like it in this hospital?"

Yes.

"Have you made friends here?"

Another definite *yes.*

"Do you like the Guardian?" Tyson was referring to the malevolent dark entity said to haunt the mirror maze and surrounding areas of the old hospital. This time, the answer was an emphatic *no.*

"Are you scared of the Guardian?"

No response.

"Are you protecting Richard?"

No.

Taking a deep breath, Richard decided to ask his own question. "Do you intend to harm me?"

The answer was immediate: *no.* He breathed a sigh of relief.

Tyson jumped back in. "Is there something in this hospital that wants to harm any of us in this room?"

Yes.

Calling out the names of every investigator present in the room, Tyson couldn't get whatever entity had been manipulating Richard to answer to any of them. Responses simply stopped coming to further questions, almost as though an "off" switch had just been flipped.

Assuming that their invisible companion had deserted them, the weary investigators turned on the lights. Sean suddenly stopped dead in his tracks.

"Look," he pointed toward a tabletop on the far side of the room. "The K-II is spiking." The K-II EMF meter, used by paranormal investigators around the world as a means of gauging localized electromagnetic fields, was pulsing and flashing, indicating the presence of an energy surge.

Sometimes such spikes are caused by cell phones either sending a text or searching for a carrier signal. The investigators were experienced and savvy enough to know this, having been burned by it before on former cases, and had all taken the precaution of switching their phones to airplane mode before beginning their experiment: they *couldn't* be transmitting. Try as they might, they couldn't find a source for the energy spikes, which died out a few moments later as quickly and mysteriously as they had arrived.

Richard and Tyson took some time to comfort Sean about his disturbing experience during the Human Pendulum experiment. "I can't explain the wave of emotion that came over me," Sean admitted, but he was already beginning to come to terms with what had happened. Maybe, he felt, it wouldn't be so bad if his grandfather *had* accompanied him to the Asylum, sort of keeping an eye on his grandson as he had once done in life.

Sean went on to tell them of a reading that he had obtained from a psychic the night before, mainly out of curiosity. The psychic had told him that the spirit of a 60-something-year-old male was following him around, and that his name was Bill. Sean had been floored by that revelation because his grandfather was in his 80s when he had just passed. His name was William.

Could some or all of this information have been obtained by the medium, via the tried and trusted methods of cold reading and the use of social media? Some of it could have, certainly, though not all.

It is also conceivable that the Human Pendulum technique can be explained by micro-muscular tremors that are controlled by the test subject's own subconscious, causing them to lean in one direction or another without being aware that they are doing it. Similar explanations have been put forward by scientists to explain the way in which the Ouija Board works.

On the other hand, an alternative explanation is that the medium was indeed in contact with Sean's dead grandfather after all. A highly skeptical Richard had sat for a reading with the same medium one day earlier, and been told that his books on the subject of the paranormal would one day soon end up as either movies or a TV series. Inwardly he had scoffed at the idea, but the smile was wiped off his face just two weeks later when a TV production company contacted him to ask about filming a show based upon some cases taken from his autobiography. Richard was on a plane to Toronto and shooting less than a month after the reading had taken place.

Was it coincidence? Perhaps . . . and perhaps not.

The possibility had to be considered that Sean's grandfather had influenced Sean by pushing him gently in order to answer those questions. If so, then its answers about having traveled to Asylum 49 along with Sean, with the express purpose of keeping him safe, made sense. But what of the spirit that had told Richard that it had followed him from Waverly Hills, and had *not* known him before it had passed away?

During the psychic reading, Richard had been told that somewhere in the region of 40 to 50 spirits sometimes followed him around, remnants of his many years investigating haunted locations; he seemed to have picked them up like the hull of a boat picks up barnacles: but, claimed the psychic, they were kept at bay by an older female figure who acted as a protector, not letting them get near him to cause any mischief.

On reflection, Richard concluded that this description might fit either his mother or one of his grandmothers, as all of them were now dead. But that wasn't what his gut was telling him, and it certainly didn't fit with some of the answers that had been given during the Human Pendulum experiment.

The spirit had claimed to have followed Richard from Waverly Hills, and had come to the Asylum with him. It had not answered when asked if more than one spirit was following him, but had made it clear that it had not known him during its lifetime, and that it only knew him after it had passed away. It claimed to like being at the old hospital and said that it had made friends there, and went on to add that although it was not protecting him, neither did it mean him any harm.

That didn't sound like a family member or a loved one to him: It seemed like more of a "spiritual hanger-on" of some sort.

There was now another possibility that Sean and Richard had to contemplate, one that was far less pleasant in nature: What if the entity or entities that had attempted to communicate with them were not who they said they were? Why should their answers be taken at face value?

Most concerning of all, was some other spirit impersonating Sean's grandfather for its own purposes?

5

The Spirits of Rooms One and Two

During the ghost hunting season, most of the haunted house attraction is taken down and the building is returned to its original state as a hospital (although it is no longer capable of caring for real patients). The former patient rooms each have a pair of hospital beds left in place, with white sheets neatly spread over the vinyl mattresses, separated by a night stand between them. In the corner of the rooms sits a comfortable chair, waiting in silent anticipation of visitors who will never come.

Rooms One and Two look no different than any of the others, at first glance; yet they *are* different, because they are inhabited by the spirits of a rambunctious little boy named Thomas, and that of a sassy elderly woman who goes by the name of Eva.

Room Two sits directly across the main hallway from the Nursery entrance, and at the time of the investigation was being used primarily for storage—mostly beds, which came with the hospital and were pushed back to back until just about every spare inch of space was crammed. One is forced to wonder just how many patients breathed their last breath on each of these beds, and taking that idea one step further, how many of them never actually left afterward.

The owners and staff at Asylum 49 are by now more than used to the strange and mysterious goings-on around the hospital, but every so often an experience stands out in their memory. This is usually because it offers an insight into the personality or quirkiness of one of the resident ghosts. Just as with the living, spirits sometimes tend to relate to and resonate with only a few people at first, as was the case with young Thomas.

Dusty Kingston, one of the owners of Asylum 49, was the first to encounter Thomas. Although she couldn't actually *see* him, Dusty believes that she frequently felt the young lad holding her hands or tugging at her clothing in an attempt to get some attention. She describes the feeling as being "cold and electric," and felt such a psychic connection with him that she brought him a Thomas the Train toy for him to play with.

A number of the sensitives and psychic mediums who had come to conduct ghost hunts at the Asylum often claimed to see him hanging around Dusty, and yet none of the other staff members or owners had experiences with him. Thomas seemed drawn to her somehow, as though the two were joined by an invisible but very tangible bond.

But it didn't take long for Thomas to start pulling pranks on the others.

It was a night like any other night at Asylum 49 when Kimm set about his usual routine of walking through the hospital hallways and rooms, stopping only to straighten up some props here and make a bed or two there. The patient rooms needed to look presentable in preparation for an upcoming ghost tour.

When they are running the ghost tours, the staff members divide up larger groups of visitors into several smaller groups, and then conduct a few rounds of tours until everybody has gotten a feel for the place and has had the opportunity to ask any questions they might have; finally, the visitors are allowed to go off on their own to investigate whichever areas of the hospital may have taken their interest.

On this particular night, the first group went through the tour circuit without anything noteworthy happening. Following along behind them, Kimm was surprised to find that all of the sheets on the patient beds were tousled and rumpled. Grumbling about the general lack of courtesy and consideration that had been shown for their fellow visitors by the first group, he returned the beds to some semblance of their made-up state.

Then the second group went through on their tour. Following behind at a respectful distance, Kimm stuck his head into the patient rooms along the maternity hall.

Yet again, the sheets were a mess.

Somebody was obviously playing games with him, and Kimm was less than amused.

Wanting to nip this little drama in the bud, Kimm decided to ask the staff members whether they had seen anybody messing up the sheets on the bed. They all shook their heads: Nobody had noticed anybody going into any of the patient rooms. Frowning, he asked a staff member to accompany him on a whirlwind trip through the maternity rooms in order to make all the beds *yet again* before the next tour group came around.

The next tour duly started, making their way slowly and methodically from room to room. Kimm already had a sneaking suspicion as to what would be found when they got to the patient rooms, as evidenced by a sinking feeling that was now developing in the pit of his stomach.

Sure enough, once the groups reached the first patient rooms along the main hallway, once again the beds had been unmade, their sheets rumpled and tossed aside. Kimm just walked away, shaking his head in disbelief.

As time passed, the tours continued to grow in popularity, mostly through word of mouth. Sometimes the beds would unmake themselves, whereas at other times they would remain pristine and unmolested. Nothing odd was showing up on the security cameras, and though none covered the beds directly, they did verify that nobody was entering or leaving the rooms apart from the guides and visitors.

The mystery of the beds remained unsolved, until one day a psychic medium contacted the Andersens out of the blue and requested permission to walk through the Asylum in order to help identify any earthbound spirits that might be haunting the hospital.

Shrugging, they figured: *Why not?* They scheduled a date and time that worked for both parties, just a few days later.

When the mutually agreed-upon date arrived, the Andersens met with the medium at the main entrance of the old hospital. They started the tour in silence, simply allowing the medium to do her own thing, being especially careful to keep from feeding her any facts or stories about the history of either the hospital or the haunting.

Once they got to the maternity hall, the small party entered the Nursery area first. It didn't take long for the medium to make contact with a spirit that she claimed was haunting the area.

"There's a little boy named Thomas in here," the medium began, "and he keeps mentioning *sheets*. Does that mean anything to you?"

Kimm thought about it for a moment, and then asked the medium whether she was talking about the old divider sheets that used to hang from metal rails running along the ceiling. The medium shook her head.

"No, not those. Are there any beds with sheets on them?"

Kimm replied that there were indeed sheets on the hospital beds that were located in the patient rooms along the hallway.

"Thomas says he likes it when you make all the beds so he can jump on them and mess them up," the medium laughed. She went on to say that Thomas was from a family of Tooele's early settlers, and that although he had died as an old man, he much preferred to show himself to a select few Asylum 49 staff as a child, reveling in the freedom of childlike behaviors.

The mystery of the messed-up beds appeared to be solved. The psychic went on to say that Thomas stayed in and around Room One of the maternity section of the main hallway for most of the time, but also sometimes wandered throughout the Labor and Delivery area whenever the fancy took him.

Now that there was a name associated with the ghost stories, Asylum 49 staff members and visiting paranormal investigators started asking for Thomas by name during their EVP sessions. Shortly thereafter, he began learning to communicate with the living by making use of the ghost hunting equipment that investigators brought along with them to the hospital.

One of his favorite games seems to be playing with their flashlights; during the ghost tours, it is standard practice for the tour guides to go out and investigate along with the guests in order to help them collect their own evidence. Generally speaking, the spirits are much more willing to communicate when one of the staff members they are familiar with is involved, perhaps because it removes an element of "stranger danger" from the mix.

One evening, Kimm was wandering around the hospital during an overnight investigation when he noticed a group of around 10 people, all clustered inside Room One. As he ducked in the room, trying to be as unobtrusive as possible, the whole place was suddenly lit up by a barrage of camera flashes that created a bright white strobe effect, which threatened to white-out his retinas. There, in the far corner of the room, he saw the form of a little boy, starkly illuminated each time the cameras strobed.

One of the visitors noticed that Kimm had jumped as though he had been startled, and so he quickly explained that he had just seen a little boy in there with them; Kimm then went on to tell the story of young Thomas and the messed-up sheets.

Up until that point, the group hadn't been getting any responses, and so Kimm carefully placed a flashlight on top of one of the rumpled patient beds. Still there was no response.

One of the female visitors in the group suggested that maybe it was because the beds weren't made. Thinking that perhaps she might be on to something, Kimm spoke up and tried to make a deal with Thomas; he promised that if Thomas would just turn on the flashlight, then he would come back the next day and make up all of the beds just for Thomas to jump up and down on.

The group waited in silence.

Suddenly, there came a distinct scratching sound on the vinyl mattress. No more than a second after that, everybody heard the definite sound of something hitting the mattress with great force. The group watched in incredulous fascination as the flashlight bounced almost a foot into the air, turned itself on, then somehow flew off the bed and clattered onto the floor.

Thomas had kept his half of the bargain. The next day, Kimm kept his own side of the deal, returning to the maternity hall and laboriously making up each of the patient beds for Thomas to mess up again. It has since become something of a game between the two, for Thomas continues to roam the hospital halls at the time of writing, and has even deigned to pose outside of Room One in order to have his picture taken.

x x x x x

For the past few years, sightings of an elderly woman sitting in a chair in the corner of Room Two have been reported on numerous occasions by staff and visitors alike. Each brief encounter would always go the same way: As the witness was walking by Room Two, they would suddenly come to a dead stop, and then peer deeply into the dark interior of the room as though searching for something. They had glimpsed a human figure out of the corner of their eye, or had caught sight of a head peeking out of the doorway of Room Two, seemingly looking up and down the length of the hallway.

The identity of this apparition remained a complete mystery until very recently, when a gentleman attending a ghost tour claimed to be capable of reading the energies contained within that room and of being able to give more detail.

Partway through the tour, the sensitive visitor stopped in the doorway and announced that he was looking at an elderly woman who had short gray hair. Kimm and Cami asked him whether he could discern her name, and hopefully a few more verifiable details about her. Frowning, he focused his attention and after a pause, finally said that the lady's name began with the letter "E" but that he couldn't make out her full name.

He threw out a few suggestions of what he thought that it *might* be, but admitted that he wasn't entirely sure—perhaps Eva, or Edith? The man paused for a moment, tilting his head as though he was listening to an invisible voice speaking into his ear, and then suddenly he began to laugh. He made a comment that the ghostly lady was a sassy one, and claimed that she had told him that she would like to get a little more recognition around here—not *too* much, she emphasized, but at least a little.

The Andersens asked him to please elaborate on what the ghostly lady meant by the phrase "a little but not too much." He described her as the type of person that very much enjoys having the company of visitors, but only for a short time. She didn't like her guests to outstay their welcome, and so simply mentioning her during future tours would be more than sufficient; a polite nod to her presence, acknowledging that Room Two was *her* room, and she would be happy.

There is a policy among the staff at Asylum 49 that both the living and the dead shall be treated with the utmost respect. With this being the case, Kimm and Cami really wanted to know whether they could get the phantom patient anything that would make her time pass more comfortably or enjoy-ably. Her reply, as relayed through the visiting sensitive, was that she very much liked to play card games, and would appreciate if she was to be given a deck of playing cards, along with a nice comfortable pillow.

The Andersens looked at one another in puzzlement. *What would a ghost want with a pillow?* Then they shrugged. A gift was a gift, no matter its ques-tionable utility value, and if that was what the old lady wanted, they would be more than happy to accommodate her. True to the woman's wishes, they left and used various items in Room Two, attempting to play card games with its ghostly occupant.

One technique that is commonly used by paranormal investigators as a means to attempt communication with the dead is known as "the flash-light trick." This entails taking a Maglite-style flashlight, switching it on, and unscrewing the head just enough that the light goes out—this breaks the electrical circuit by separating connector wires in the body and head of the light. Then one invites any entities that may be present to speak by causing it to light up in response to questions; the theory goes that discarnate spirits are able to either paranormally bring those connectors into contact with one another, or to supply a small amount of additional energy in order to make the flashlight illuminate.

There are those who are skeptical of the flashlight trick, pointing out that when one uses such a device, parts of it will inevitably heat up, which in turn can cause expansion inside the flashlight and thereby give false-positive readings. An alternative technique is to use a flashlight *without* unscrewing the lens at its head, and request any spirits present to make the beam flicker a specific number of times.

Misty and Cami attempted to use the flashlight trick to indulge in Eva's favorite pastime of playing cards. Sweeping the beam over the hand of cards that they had dealt for the dead woman, they requested that Eva blink the light once it was shining on the specific card that she wanted to play.

This worked for the first couple of hands, but then the energy in the room seemed to dissipate. The card players tried again several more times. Unfortunately, they would never be able to get more than two or three turns into a game before the mysterious ghostly resident of Room Two seemed to lose interest.

The visit was not without its successes, however: Soon after the abortive attempt to play cards with her, Misty was able to expand upon the limited information available about the elderly woman who haunts Room Two. Misty was keen to learn a little more about her, particularly anything that might help shed light on her actual identity.

It wasn't long before she was able to psychically discern a lady's name: Edith.

As time goes on, the staff and owners of Asylum 49 continue to carry out research and conduct further investigations into identities and characteristics of the ghosts who haunt the old hospital. They are slowly but surely gathering more information with which to fill in the gaps, and have high hopes that one day they will have finally gathered enough pieces of the jigsaw to allow them to complete the entire picture. They are well aware of the fact that these spirits were once living, breathing people, and that during their lifetimes they were loved by friends, children, grandchildren, mothers, fathers, and siblings alike. Few people wish to be forgotten after their passing, and the Asylum 49 staff is committed to not only treating their resident spirits with the greatest of respect, but also to share some of their stories with those who continue to encounter them at the hospital today.

Photo of the front main hospital entrance.

One day, Cami received a message from a young lady who lives in Colorado. She happened to be traveling to Tooele in order to visit friends and family during the Christmas season, and claimed to have been born in the old hospital during its heyday. Would it be possible, she wondered, for her to set up a time to meet with somebody at the hospital, so that she could show her two young children the place where she had been born? For her part, Cami was more than happy to allow the visit. The two women went back and forth until settling upon a meeting time, which happened to be on Christmas Eve, early in the afternoon.

They met at the Emergency Room entrance on the south side of the hospital. The pair shook hands, made introductions, and entered the old building together, accompanied by the lady's children. The wide-eyed kids fired off a barrage of questions as they went, covering anything and everything they found to be of interest; their mother and Cami talked about the history of the hospital itself, discussing the function of each area that they passed through, focusing upon what had taken place there when the hospital was still operating. It transpired that the family had all seen the episode featuring Asylum 49 on *Ghost Adventures*, where lead investigator Zak Bagans and his team had carried out an investigation of the building.

Where were the ghosts most active, the family wanted to know, and what were the TV stars like in real life? This led to even more questions about the Asylum's various ghosts, and so Cami decided to give them all a full-on ghost tour: She kept it child-friendly, of course, leaving out some of the more gruesome or frightening aspects.

When they finally reached Room Two, Cami told them that there was said to be the spirit of a sassy yet sweet elderly tenant still haunting the room—the ghost of a grey-haired old lady who likes visitors (though not for long periods of time), enjoys playing cards, and whose name began with the letter "E."

Cami watched as the woman's eyes grew wide and she turned pale, an expression bordering on shock slowly crossing her face. Quietly, the visiting lady said, "I think this is the room that my grandmother stayed in. Her name was Eva and she liked to play pinochle every single day. I loved her dearly and have missed her every second since she died."

Slowly, she walked across the threshold into Room Two, and waited at the foot of the hospital bed that now stood closest to the doorway, seeming to gather her thoughts. Taking a deep breath, she recounted the memory of having stood in that exact same spot and looking at her grandmother as she lay there, dying in the bed.

"You can talk to her, you know," Cami told her gently. "If she *is* your grandmother, perhaps you could ask her to give you a sign to show us that she is present, and that she is truly your grandmother Eva."

Nodding, the visitor asked for some kind of sign or indication. Nothing happened. Undeterred, the woman continued to speak as if her grandmother was actually there in the room with them.

Not knowing whether the ghost of Room Two was in residence today or not, Cami nonetheless decided to give grandmother and granddaughter some private time alone together. "Take as much time as you need," she said, slipping back out into the hallway. "I'll be right outside."

Cami waited a respectful distance outside the room. Inside Room Two, the visitor talked to the spirit of her grandmother, telling stories to her children of the many happy times that they had spent together. Her voice cracked from time to time, full of heartfelt love and longing. Cami was struck with the realization of just what an honor it was to bear witness to such a beautiful event, and a lump began to form in her throat as the lady continued to reminisce. She wiped a tear from her eye when the family came outside into the hallway, their one-sided conversation now finished.

Although she never did get a clear-cut sign that it was actually her grandmother's spirit haunting Room Two, she had somehow become certain that it was truly her. Cami remained open-minded on the matter, and suggested that if it really was the case, then her grandmother might well choose to give her a sign to prove it, in a way that only she could recognize.

"So pay attention," Cami reminded her with a smile as they parted company in the parking lot. "You never know when—or *how*—a message might come through . . ."

"I'll send you a picture of my grandmother," the lady promised. "Show it to anybody who sees the spirit in Room Two, so that we can see if it really is the same person."

True to her word, later that evening she sent Cami a family picture with her grandmother in it. The picture had names identifying who was who, and which row they could be found sitting or standing in. She also sent along a portrait-style photo of just her grandmother. The woman in the photo looked like anybody's grandmother might look: an elderly lady with beautiful, sparkling eyes that looked back at Cami from cat's eye-framed decorative metal glasses.

During the writing process for this book, Cami wanted to clarify the name of the ghostly lady from Room Two. For some reason, she had gotten it into her head that her name may have been either Edna or Edith, rather than Eva—perhaps because Edith was the name that Misty had picked up on when she had first entered Room Two.

Cami wrote to the lady's granddaughter in Colorado, asking her to settle the question. A reply soon came, saying that although her grandmother's name was indeed Eva, her own mother's name (which would have been Eva's daughter) happened to be . . . Edith.

She went on to tell Cami that she was really glad that the Asylum 49 owner had reached out to her, because she had very recently had a very sweet, rather beautiful dream in which she had been reunited with her grandmother once more.

Was it a coincidence that the name initially heard by Misty happened to be Edith, which turned out to be the name of the daughter of the woman who had spent her final days in Room Two? Perhaps; it's impossible to say for sure. Cami decided to take things one step further, and sent the portrait photo of Eva to Misty, asking her whether she recognized the woman who was its subject. She did not make any mention of her conversation, wanting to see what would happen.

"Oh my God, Cami, that's the elderly woman in Room Two!" was her excited response. "Where on Earth did you get that picture?"

6

The Secret of Room 666

Room Six was no longer known as Room Six. This is because an extra pair of number sixes had been painted on the door front, renaming it Room 666 in order to fit in with the generally demonic theme of the main hallway. Thousands of customers had been made to jump out of their skin when they passed by its open doorway in the semi-darkness, only to be confronted by a wizened, skeletal old man in a wheelchair that was being pushed along by a zombie nurse.

These two terrifying figures were, of course, fake, mere illusions cooked up by the special effects crew. The main reason to fear Room 666 was something altogether different . . . and *real*.

Staff at the Asylum didn't call it 666 at all. They simply knew it as "Westley's Room."

Westley had been a long-term resident at the Asylum back in its hospital days, and Room Six had been his. Tragically, Westley had suffered from that cruelest of medical conditions, Alzheimer's disease. Like many such unfortunate souls, Westley had both his good days and his bad days, depending upon the progression of his illness.

On good days, he was both friendly and well-intentioned; on the bad, he could be aggressive, violent, and combative. A sketch of Westley's face hangs on the door outside his room, drawn by a visiting psychic medium. He is a somber-looking man, wide-eyed and balding. He departed this life during the 1990s, and was close to being 90 years old when he died.

Volunteers at Asylum 49 believe that his spirit never left.

The type of paranormal activity that has been reported in Westley's room varies greatly. When the Asylum staff discusses the subject amongst themselves, usually in hushed voices, many speculate that Westley's mental state is reflected in the fact that some of the activity is warm and almost friendly, whereas the rest can be downright menacing. One only has to look at the episode of *Ghost Adventures* in which lead investigator Zak Bagans was conducting an EVP session in Westley's room. Admittedly, Bagans' tone was somewhat less than respectful, and whatever entity occupied the room duly responded in kind, slamming Bagans violently against the wall and knocking the wind out of him.

When psychic medium Misty Grimstead takes visitors around the hospital, she invites them to stand in the doorway of Room 666 and to relax, clear their mind, and then ask the spirit of Westley whether he would like their company. Some feel themselves to be drawn inside, as though the lonely old occupant is welcoming them in. Others are pushed back out over the threshold, clearly signifying his desire to be left alone.

"People have been pushed and slammed in here pretty hard," says Misty, a five-year veteran of the Asylum. "We take it to mean that either they're not behaving respectfully, or that Westley's having one of his bad days. If you're smart, you get out of there fast and just leave him in peace. It's . . . *safer* that way."

Several people have experienced the violence and anger of either Westley or some other angry entity inside the confines of Room 666. More than a few shocked visitors have walked out of there with stinging welts on the surface of their skin, bright red scratches, not to mention a plethora of bruises; visitors often report experiencing feelings of intense discomfort in there, and a feeling of not being wanted inside the room, as though *somebody* wants them out.

Westley is an exceptionally strong spirit, and one that is more than willing to express himself physically. He is also a very willing participant during the frequent ghost tours, in which visitors are advised to stand at the far end of the main hallway and shine a dim flashlight beam toward the aluminum doorway that leads to the clown maze outside. The goal is to illuminate that doorway just enough to be able to see the shadowy form of Westley walk out of his room, which he tends to do quite often.

Although Westley is known to reside inside Room 666 and to cross the hallway whenever he feels like it, there are times when the behavior of the shadow figure at the end of the hallway acts in an uncharacteristically sinister way, far more aggressively than would generally be attributed to him. This obviously begs the question: Is Westley the only spirit haunting the space at the end of the hallway?

Late one night, Cami Andersen and fellow paranormal investigator Cathy Blank were in the main hallway, watching what they felt sure was Westley's shadow moving restlessly back and forth across the corridor outside of Room 666. The shadow was moving with such speed that the figure appeared somehow smeared and stretched, as though it was distorted or twisted. The two investigators discussed how odd it was for Westley to behave in such a way, and wondered what might be causing his extreme agitation.

Determined to try and find out, they began to conduct an EVP session, taking turns to ask Westley questions:

"Why are you so upset, Westley?"

"Is there someone else down there with you?"

"Will you please calm down?"

"Is there something we can do to help you relax?"

Cathy was lying on her belly and shining the dim flashlight beam down the hallway. Although the girls hadn't gotten any response to their questions, they continued watching the dark figure's frantic motions. After a while, the shadow slowly calmed itself, seeming to vanish, only to reappear farther along the hallway, closer to the two curious investigators. The shadow man would then vanish again, before reappearing back at the end of the hallway once more, where the frantic back and forth pacing would resume.

Cami and Cathy grew increasingly nervous as they watched the bizarre behavior of the shadow figure unfold, repeating its actions again and again as though stuck in some sort of time loop; each time, the entity appeared a little closer to them, before going back to the end of the hallway. Each time that the figure materialized at the far end of the hall, Cathy called out for it to remain there at the end of the hallway, close to the entrance of Room 666.

For a short time only, it would honor Cathy's request, before suddenly seeming to grow bored, and then begin inching its way toward them yet again, hugging one of the walls.

The two women giggled nervously, responding to the tension that each of them was beginning to feel. Once more, Cathy instructed it to return to the other end of the hallway. Once more, it did . . . for now.

They watched the dark mass as it stood silhouetted against the doorway at the end of the main hallway, lurking directly outside Room 666. Each of them could quite plainly see that its legs were slightly parted, and could also make out the outline of a head, supported on a thin neck and shoulders, which in turn merged into a pair of arms that hung down loosely by its sides.

Barely drawing breath, Cami and Cathy watched as the figure just stood there, seemingly staring at them as though sizing them up, in the manner of one adversary to another.

The three of them continued to stare at each other in silence. Time passed, but neither investigator wanted to move a muscle, let alone look at their watches; they simply lay there on the ground in the middle of the corridor, barely able to believe what their eyes were telling them.

Cathy considered trying for a picture, but knew from long experience that most attempts to photograph shadow figures achieved little more than scaring them away, or at best whiting out their image when the flash went off. Although some shadowy forms have been captured in photos taken at Asylum 49, most seem only visible to the naked eye, and even then are best seen during low-light conditions. Shadow figures and bright lights do not go well together.

In a move so fast that it shocked them both, the figure suddenly dropped into a crouch and began crawling toward them on all fours. Rooted to the spot, the two investigators were near-paralyzed with fear as each shuffling twitch of the shadow figure's limbs drew it closer to them. Neither spoke a word or attempted to flee, though every nerve ending was screaming at them to get up and run.

Before they knew it, the thing had reached their position and was rearing back on its legs, looming over Cathy's prostrate body. Cami got slowly to her feet, not wanting to provoke or disturb the thing, and quietly said, "Cathy, I think it's time to go. It's. Standing. *Right*. Over. You." Each word came through clenched teeth.

Taking her friend's advice, Cathy slowly stood, not knowing what would happen next. She straightened up to her full height.

The shadow figure was nowhere to be seen. It had vanished before Cami's eyes.

Not wishing to look a gift horse in the mouth, both investigators backed slowly out of the hall, neither of them willing to turn their backs on the doorway to Room 666. They had reached the dubious safety of the big white double doors and closed them behind themselves before they dared let out a sigh of relief.

It was now all too clear to the girls that it wasn't the spirit of Westley that had squared off against them in the corridor. But if it wasn't the ghostly old man, what else could possibly be haunting the vicinity of Room 666?

x x x x x

The former Room Six has been a source of great interest for many visiting paranormal investigators, and it is no different for horror movie buffs, who usually stop dead in their tracks when they catch sight of the triple 6s on the outside of the wooden door.

For many, there is an undeniable allure to the subject of demonic entities and occult symbols. Halloween is such a busy time at the old hospital that there are very rarely any ghost tours, but every once in a while an opportunity presents itself which simply cannot be passed up. Such was the case in October of 2013, a year in which Halloween night fell upon a Thursday.

Typically, the haunt attraction is in operation during the holiday season from 7 p.m. until 10 p.m. every Tuesday, Wednesday, and Thursday, with extended hours until midnight on Fridays and Saturdays. Because the haunt was due to close early enough that night, the owners decided to try something new: they would host a Halloween ghost tour. After all, they reasoned, tonight was All Hallows' Eve, when the veil between worlds was said to be thinnest, allowing the dead to cross over and visit the land of the living.

Surely the Asylum's ghostly tenants would want to take advantage of the opportunity?

As the last customers of the evening went through, Kimm and Cami quickly dismissed the cast of performers, hurriedly emptying the building in preparation for the ghost tour, which was scheduled to start at 11 p.m. Everybody present said that they felt the same thing: The energy was running high this year, and the night had thus far been a huge success. Anticipation was running equally high for Asylum 49's first ever Halloween ghost hunt.

It would not disappoint.

Although 11 o'clock might seem like a late time to start one of their ghost tours, the Andersens were pleasantly surprised to find that there were 15 die-hard ghost hunters and assorted paranormal thrill-seekers waiting in the front lobby when Cami finally said her goodbyes to the cast and thanked them for yet another night of stellar performances. Joining her for the night was long-time tour guide and resident security guard, Buck. Cami and Buck each took a group under their wing, giving them a tour of the hospital and pointing out what each area had been used for when Tooele Valley Hospital was still in business.

After the tour, the members of each group were invited to either investigate on their own, or to accompany one of the tour guides. Buck made his way to the conference room, while Cami ventured to Room 666. Unsurprisingly, most of the hardier souls present decided that they wanted to tackle the spirits of Room 666, what with this being the most ghostly night of the year.

Outside Room 666, a dozen people were sitting with their backs resting up against the wall, while one brave man sat in a recliner in the center of the room. The man claimed to be able to sense the presence of spirits, and went on to tell those assembled that he had the strong sensation that the presence lurking within Room 666 wasn't at all happy about his sitting in the chair—it really wanted him to leave.

"If you'd like me to leave, tell me to leave," said the man, almost daring the spirits to throw him out.

Nothing happened.

"I feel like you don't want me here," the man pressed on, his tone of voice taking on just a hint of challenge. "Do you not want me sitting in your chair? If not, why don't you make a noise to let me know?"

Still nothing.

He made numerous attempts to get the presence that he said he was feeling to respond to his provocation. Every time that he asked to be shown a sign in order to make him leave, nothing tangible would happen, other than his expressing just how uncomfortable he was starting to feel. The man's anxiety level ratcheted up until he felt that he was somehow in physical danger, and said that he really didn't want to provoke some sort of paranormal attack. Admitting defeat, he finally rose from the chair and joined the rest of the group outside in the hallway.

Shortly afterward, the man sat down with the rest of the group, all of them clustering directly to the side of Room 666's doorway. Suddenly, the recliner groaned and creaked as though someone had just sat down in the chair and put their full weight on the springs. Cami quickly reminded the group that not everything is paranormal in nature, and that the most likely conclusion was that an old and worn-out piece of furniture was simply settling and readjusting itself after the pressure had been taken off it.

The group listened intently to see whether any more sounds would come out of the room. The chair did indeed pop and squeak a few more times, which led Cami to suggest that they try to get a sign that someone might truly be sitting in the chair. Straining their ears in the pitch black hallway, the guest investigators waited as Cami asked for whichever spirit was now resident in Room 666 to give them some kind of sign that would let them know, beyond a shadow of a doubt, that somebody had indeed sat down in the chair.

For several minutes, no sound at all came out of Room 666, or from anywhere else within earshot for that matter. Boredom overcame one of the guests, to the point that they pulled the phone out of their pocket in order to check their e-mail. Cami was sitting directly across from the doorway of Room 666, and at that moment she happened to look up toward the door. There, in the dim glow coming from the cell phone that momentarily lit up the darkness, she saw that the door was no longer wide open, as it had been when the man that was sitting in the chair had left the room. It was now mostly closed, with only a small gap of about three inches being visible.

"Oh my gosh, guys, the door is almost completely shut!" Cami exclaimed, reaching for her flashlight and shining it directly at the mostly closed door.

Suddenly, without any warning at all, the door slammed violently shut, with such force that the sound echoed throughout the entire hospital. Even the small team who had elected to investigate the conference room heard it, and came to check on what had happened.

The group simply sat there in stunned silence for a few seconds, before bursting out in excited chatter about what had just occurred. Everyone *knew* without any doubt whatsoever that there was no living human being situated inside Room 666; they *knew* that nobody was close enough to have pulled the door shut, not to mention the fact that everyone was quite visibly sitting on the ground in plain sight; and finally, they all *knew* that they had experienced something truly inexplicable.

x x x x x

Through the years, the staff at Asylum 49 has built a diverse array of experimental equipment for use during their ghost hunts, one of which happened to be a Jacob's ladder. This device was used by Zak Bagans and the *Ghost Adventures* crew when they filmed their episode at Asylum 49, the events of which culminated inside Room 666.

A Jacob's ladder is the type of high voltage "climbing arc" display seen in many old science fiction movies, or the classic Universal monster movies, in which the device looks completely at home in the lair of any mad scientist or alien overlord. The ladder (or some variation of it) is always easy to spot, being the strange-looking device that is usually found lurking somewhere in the background and has an electrical arc rising and pulsing between two steel rods. This electromagnetic activity gives off an eerie electrostatic sound, and also creates a rather spectacular visual effect, thanks to the high-voltage transformer that powers it.

The Asylum 49 staff built their own version of the Jacob's ladder in an attempt to enhance their efforts to communicate with the spirits that haunt their building. They wanted to test the theory that spirits are a form of pure energy, and that therefore, in order to manifest, they must need a large amount of energy to serve as a power source. Once the device is placed in a room or other area of the Asylum, it is switched on and then left to charge the room in the hopes that a greater amount of paranormal activity and communication will occur.

Sometimes this does indeed turn out to be the case.

Tyson Lemmon was investigating with a group in Room 666, and had opted to use the Jacob's ladder in order to try and increase the likelihood of paranormal activity taking place. Some of the group members were standing against the windows along the south end of the room, while Tyson and a few others stood with their backs to the east wall.

"We were sitting there watching the doorway because, you know, we had a feeling that someone was watching us," Tyson explains. "All at once, we saw a pair of bright red eyes appear in there, about four feet off the ground. We were really freaked out, but we tried to keep calm."

The red eyes vanished just a few seconds later, but the group gamely continued to investigate: They attempted to get the owner of the red eyes to come back for the next 30 minutes, despite the fact that, deep down, some of the investigators wondered whether they really did in fact *want* them to come back.

The small group continued to watch the doorway of Room 666, not knowing what to expect, when they saw a pair of white circles (which some of the observers felt may also have been eyes) hovering roughly six feet above the ground, giving the eerie impression that some mostly unseen entity was peering back into the room at them.

Then the white orbs simply disappeared.

Understandably a little freaked out by the experience, Tyson and his team left Room 666 to its own devices, practically stampeding out into the main hallway.

The loud *bang* took everybody by surprise, making even the most seasoned of the investigators jump.

"What the hell was that?" Tyson wanted to know, bringing his flashlight around to cover the far end of the hallway, down toward the nurses' station.

There he found his answer; for where the big double doors had been propped open all night, he saw that they had suddenly both just been slammed shut, leaving him and his group isolated in a dark and abandoned corridor.

x x x x x

It was coming up to midnight on the Sunday after Halloween of 2015 when Richard Estep and his team elected to conduct a spirit box session in the doorway to Westley's room. The "spirit box" is a radio frequency scanner, which hops from frequency to frequency (either forward or backward, depending on how the operator sets it up) and provides fragments of white noise through which, some investigators believe, discarnate entities can manifest their voices.

Richard remained in the security center some 200 feet further down the hall, watching over his teammates by way of the CCTV monitors, while Sean, Jennifer, Autumn, Randy, Catlyn, Jen, and Robbin clustered around the spirit box in the corridor directly outside Room 666. Having killed the lights in both the corridor and the patient rooms, the seven investigators now stood within a pool of deep shadow, clustered around the device that may be a communication channel to the spirit world. Robbin flicked on the power switch with her thumb.

With a crackle and hiss, the spirit box came to life and began to scan through a range of radio frequencies. The investigators took turns asking questions, and when answers came, they would be delivered in short, staccato bursts of human voices. Some of the responses were simply spoken conversationally, whereas others had such a musical quality about them that they were almost *sung*; still others were barely intelligible at all, and in the end had to be dismissed as plain old white noise.

The session began with the team asking the usual questions: Were there any spirit entities present? Did they want to come forward and communicate, or at least try to make their presence known?

Stay back, a male voice from the box squawked immediately.

"Do you want Robbin to stay back?" Sean asked, speaking to the box, but watching his colleague standing in the doorway who was holding it.

By the wall.

Robbin refused to move. The next utterance from the box was a single, very profane word, that caused a disbelieving Sean to exclaim, "Did it just call you the *C-word*?!?"

"Hey, hey, hey, *hey*, HEY!" Robbin barked, refusing to be insulted. Some of the investigators winced, not only at the obscenity spoken by the box, but instinctively at the sound of Robbin's "mom voice." It would be a brave entity indeed that was willing to lock horns with her. Some of the investigators were not sure that they had heard the slur, however, and it would be the subject of much debate at the end of the night.

Back up, came a voice, followed seconds later by a different one that told the investigator to *get out.* Quietly, Sean ducked out to fetch Richard, who he felt sure would want to hear the intelligent responses coming from the box at first hand.

"Say my name," Robbin challenged the unseen entities, but no sooner were the words out of her mouth than a male voice said through the box: *bend over.* Blushing but undeterred, Robbin instead stepped further into the darkness of Room 666, making room for Richard to take her old position in the doorway.

"Who's this gentleman standing in the door?" Sean called out. The reply was quite faint, but seemed to say the word *idiot.* Now it was Richard's turn to blush, while his fellow investigators could barely stifle their grins.

"Who do you want to back off?" Sean continued. *Robbin* was the response, spoken twice in what seemed to be two different voices. Blinking in surprise, Sean poked his head around the doorframe. All that he could see inside was darkness. "Who's in there?"

Wes, responded a male voice just an instant later.

The investigators looked at one another, visibly impressed. These were lucid, intelligent responses to direct questioning, something that wasn't always experienced when using the spirit box.

Estep came next, which made Richard's blood run cold.

"Could you say Richard's last name again, please?" Sean asked politely. His courtesy was snubbed when a male voice replied with the word *asshole.*

Less than thrilled with his new nickname, Richard asked whether the entities present wanted the team to stay in there or to go. *Get out,* came the prompt answer, sung back to him by a male voice. "What's her name?" Richard pressed, pointing to Autumn. The response was difficult to make out: it may or may not have said Autumn's name.

When a supposed EVP is difficult to make out, the wise investigator discards it as potential evidence on the grounds that it is more likely to be random white noise than anything paranormal. So it would have been with this particular response, except for the fact that when Sean asked "Did I just hear 'Autumn'?" a male voice immediately piped up with *You did.*

Suddenly, Richard had regained his popularity—either that or another spirit was chiming in. *Richard,* a masculine voice said, *I love you.*

Richard took a step back in surprise. His mind went back to the psychic reading that he had requested a few nights earlier, and he recalled the medium's description of a strong female spirit who watched over him affectionately, like a protector. Could this perhaps be the same entity, trying to communicate with him via the spirit box? If so, why did the voice sound more male than female?

Robbin was adamant that the voice had spoken with a British accent, although Richard wasn't sure that he could hear it himself.

The entire team was embarrassed at what the spirit box said next.

Spank you.

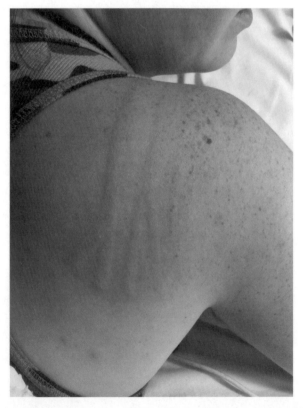

Scratches that appeared on Autumn's shoulder after a disturbing spirit box session, which was held in doorway of Room 666.

They looked at one another and mouthed the words incredulously. What were they dealing with here—some kind of ghostly pervert?

"Who do you want to spank?" Sean insisted. There was no response at first, but when the question was repeated, a mellifluous voice (which sounded quite feminine) came back with: *Robbin.*

Sean actually sounded disappointed with that answer, and asked the entity whether it would rather spank Richard. The answer was an unequivocal *NO.*

"This isn't a great night for me," Richard whispered under his breath. "Not only am I apparently now an a-hole, but I'm apparently not even remotely spankable either."

Despite the atmosphere of both excitement and tension that resulted from this interaction with unseen voices, Sean now had a mischievous glint in his eye. "You want to spank Richard, don't you?" he smirked, not really expecting an answer to the flippant question. After a five-second delay, a male voice answered calmly: *Not so much.*

The sun was just coming up when the team decided to call it a night. Heading back to his hotel room, Richard was just about to flop down on the bed and grab some much-needed sleep when a ping from his phone indicated an incoming text message. It was from Jennifer.

"This just turned up on Autumn's back," the text read. Beneath that single line was a picture of Autumn's right shoulder. Three long, angry scratches had appeared there, upraised welts that looked a lot like claw marks from some kind of animal. Jen had first noticed them when her daughter had taken off her jacket before showering.

"Do they hurt, honey?" Jen had asked, worried for her daughter's safety.

"No, Mom," Autumn shook her head. "I can't feel anything."

"No itchiness? Burning?" As a seasoned paramedic, Jen took off her mom hat and fell straight into her professional mode of thinking. Autumn shook her head again, repeating that the marks were completely painless.

Staring at the image of Autumn's shoulder on his phone, Richard was every bit as shocked as Jennifer and Autumn were. Despite the early hour, he decided to consult with his go-to priest, a professional cellist and ordained Catholic named Stephen Weidner. Stephen was a seasoned paranormal investigator himself, and had even brought his own team to the Asylum in the past: they had left with some truly impressive results, and were eager to return. In fact, Stephen would have been physically present with the Boulder-based team tonight had professional commitments not prevented it.

"Look at the bifurcated ends," Stephen answered immediately, remarkable considering it was almost dawn. The priest was very much a night owl. "I don't want to worry you, but the way they split like that. It usually means that they're the work of something dark—possibly even demonic . . ."

7

Births and Deaths

In hospitals all around the world, Labor and Delivery is a place of hard-won joy most of the time. For as long as humanity has existed, the natural process of childbirth has always involved blood, sweat, and no small amount of agony. The reward at the end of this age-old struggle almost always involves tears. Most often, those tears are tears of joy from the exhausted but victorious mother, and are echoed by the tears of gratitude and relief from both family members and well-wishing friends.

But as with so much else in life, childbirth also has a darker side. The miracle of modern medicine has reduced the risk of complication and mortality to the lowest that it has ever been at any time in human history, and yet still there is the risk of death for mother and child when things go wrong, as they still sometimes do, even today.

What can be said for sure is that, while the vast majority of deliveries conducted in the Labor and Delivery wing of the Tooele Valley Hospital went well and resulted in healthy children being delivered into the arms of eagerly waiting parents, there would still have been those few instances in which things took a turn for the worse. Mothers or babies—sometimes, even more tragically, *both*—would have died in there, most of them within the Labor and Delivery ward.

Needless to say, it has its ghosts.

The shadow figure of a huge male, estimated to be some seven feet tall, has been sighted in here by multiple visitors to the Asylum. Although his behavior is not usually particularly threatening (he opts to simply stand behind the nurses' station and observe), he is not always silent, sometimes choosing to make his voice heard during EVP sessions by either calling out the names of some of those present, or as on one particularly memorable occasion, uttering the chilling request: *Come here.*

Misty Grimstead claims to have spoken with a nurse named either Eve or Eva, who is found going about her duties as she did during her lifetime. It was strange, Misty said, in that it seemed as though she had encountered a simple case of a residual haunting, and yet she was having an intelligent conversation with the nurse.

"She doesn't know that she's dead," Misty explains, before going on to describe the nurse. She has short dark hair and seems to be in her late 30s to mid-40s, standing at somewhere around 5'2" and is clothed in an old-fashioned white nurse's uniform dress.

One of the more tragic spirits that is said to haunt Labor and Delivery is a young lady by the name of Emma (not her real name). Emma was a teen-ager who died in childbirth along with her newborn baby, sometime during the 1960s. Unsurprisingly, when psychic mediums reach out to Emma in order to try and comfort her, she is often inconsolable and can do little more than cry her heart out.

On those occasions during which her ghost was sighted, it was most often seen sitting hunched in the corner of the room, disconsolately weeping and rocking back and forth. As of 2015, this portion of Labor and Delivery has been converted into a fake morgue, complete with an autopsy dissection table upon which a fake cadaver lays, filleted wide open and thoroughly gut-ted; what appear to be body locker doors are set into a false free-standing wall, which completely covers that particular area.

It is something of an open secret among the Asylum 49 staff and tour guides that Emma sometimes has a very real physical effect upon female visitors who happen to be either pregnant, have recently given birth, or have recently miscarried. On multiple occasions, such visitors—who usually tend to disregard the warnings given to them about touring the Labor and

Delivery wing—suddenly find themselves overcome with intense emotion, bursting into tears without any apparent cause. Sometimes the unfortunate mothers break down completely, sinking to the ground with their heads in their hands, reduced to a sobbing, traumatized wreck.

It should be pointed out that these incidents never happen to male visitors, and have afflicted women who had not been told about the sad story of Emma and her terrible loss.

"It's always the same," says Kimm. "They're always pregnant, or have just been pregnant, and it's always in the same place—the far end of Labor and Delivery where Emma is seen. We try and keep them out of there if it looks like they could be carrying a baby, but they don't always want to listen. Then, usually they wish that they *had*."

Often, the distressed female visitors will simply leave, cutting their visit short in order to compose themselves again. Is it possible that they are

This area once echoed with the cries of women in labor and those of newborn babies . . . and sometimes still does.

psychically picking up on Emma's emotional distress and are establishing an empathic connection of some kind with the poor girl's spirit?

Passing through the autopsy room, one enters a narrow tunnel filled with body bags that are hanging from meat hooks. They may look a little cheesy by the light of the day, but in the darkness this passageway has a genuinely eerie feeling, particularly as the visitor is forced to elbow and shoulder their way through the hanging corpses to get to the next portion of Labor and Delivery: the crematorium.

A huge wall of frosted glass looks out onto the outside world. Although a large furnace dominates the center of the room nowadays, it actually once served as the surgical suite for the Labor and Delivery department. The appa-rition of a surgeon has been seen in this room at least once by two witnesses during a ghost hunt, both of whom tried vainly to bring up their cameras and snap a photo before the figure disappeared in the blink of an eye.

Residual noises are also heard in here, usually those common to the day-to-day operation of any hospital, including the beeping of heart monitors and the hushed voices of doctors and nurses in consultation with one another.

Tyson and Julie Lemmon have spent nine years working at Asylum 49, and have amassed many stories during that time; and yet none stands out quite as much in their minds as their very first paranormal experience, which took place within the walls of the Labor and Delivery department.

Conducting an informal ghost hunt with two of their close friends one evening, the four made their way carefully along the length of the main cor-ridor and turned left into one of the former delivery rooms. Standing in a hud-dle just outside the nurses' station, they watched in astonishment as a shadowy black figure paced quietly back and forth just beyond the inner doorway.

In a brave (some might say foolhardy) attempt to catch the figure by sur-prise, one of the four investigators circled around via the back entrance to the Labor and Delivery rooms. At the same time, the remaining three stepped out into the open in order to confront it directly. The figure vanished immediately, seeming to disappear into thin air, but then the group shushed one another as a faint noise could now be heard from the main hallway outside: the sound of sprinting footsteps, rapidly disappearing toward the far end of the corridor.

Dashing outside, Tyson and Julie found the corridor to be completely deserted.

The small group discussed the situation, and quickly agreed upon a strategy. They would sit in the main hallway immediately outside Labor and Delivery, and try to establish contact with the shy spirit that they had apparently frightened away just a few moments before.

Being relatively new to the field of paranormal investigation, they had little in the way of even the most basic equipment, and so the four simply sat there and talked in hushed, respectful tones, allowing the atmosphere to settle down a little.

Suddenly, the silence was shattered by the sound of a loud bang. Four heads jerked around in an effort to see where it had originated from, which seemed to be one of the abandoned patient rooms further along the hallway. Getting to their feet and going to investigate, Julie and Tyson soon found the source of the bang: a fake tombstone, used as a prop during the haunt, had been hurled out of its room and had fallen into the main corridor.

"It was just Styrofoam, so it really shouldn't have made much noise," Tyson reflected later, "but it hit that wall like a *brick*. We all freaked out and hauled ass *out* of there! It was the first time I'd ever seen a shadow person."

To this day, Tyson unapologetically tells anybody who asks that the Labor and Delivery department is his favorite part of the building, hands down. When asked why, he will enthusiastically tell of the time that he was helping to construct a new prop for that particular part of the hospital. Setting down his hammer on the ground at his side for just a moment, he reached for it again, only to feel his fingers close on empty air. Looking down, he saw with a frown that the hammer was gone: it had somehow been moved clear across the room, and now leaned tauntingly against the far wall, silently challenging him to explain how it had ended up there.

Julie Lemmon has less of a soft spot for Labor and Delivery. During one of the earlier haunts at Asylum 49, she noticed that the stretch of corridor outside the former birthing center looked much too clean and sterile for part of a haunted house. The performers who would ply their trade in that particular part of the building were going to be playing the roles of supernatural asylum patients, which hardly fit with the context of a neat and tidy corridor.

Deciding to dirty things up a little, Julie went outside and gathered up some black dust and a little dirt from the ground. Smearing handfuls of it across the walls and leaving filthy smears, Julie stepped back for a moment to admire her handiwork: Yes, she thought with approval, that was more like it! Things were starting to look suitably gross and disgusting now. With a satisfied nod, she went outside to scoop up a few more handfuls of dust and dirt.

When she returned to finish the job, Julie suddenly stopped dead in her tracks, utterly stunned by what now awaited her. Totally forgotten, the dirt trickled from her slack fingers.

She had only been gone a short time, and yet the sheets and mattresses had been stripped from all of the patient beds and tossed into the corridor outside Labor and Delivery, where they were stacked in a rough, untidy heap.

Julie felt that somebody was trying to send her a message, one which she was hearing loud and clear: *Stop making a mess and disrespecting our home . . . or else!*

8

Chapel of the Damned

What was once the hospital conference room is now virtually unrecognizable as such. In 2015, the big wooden table that was left over from its days of hosting meetings and committees was removed as part of the plan to convert the conference room into a faux chapel, albeit one with decidedly terrifying overtones.

It is also one of the most paranormally active locations in the entire hospital.

Stained-glass scenes from the life of Jesus Christ adorn the walls. Far from being props, the glass windows are genuine, purchased from an old European church by the owners of Asylum 49. A lectern stands at one end, and facing it are several rows of pews. Sitting on each pew are two or three ghostly figures in flowing white robes, giving the impression of a congregation of the dead that is waiting silently and patiently for some paranormal pastor to begin their unholy sermon. More than one member of the staff has reported seeing the mannequins swaying and moving, as though manipulated by some unseen force; this occurs when the air inside the chapel is completely still, with no drafts or breezes blowing through the building.

Some of the benches in the chapel were made from scratch by the Asylum 49 construction crew, but others were genuine second-hand church pews that were snapped up from a consignment store. Further investigation into their history revealed that the pews had been obtained from a mortuary that was located next door to that particular shop.

Paranormal investigators soon learned that an earthbound male spirit was attached to one of the pews; this was supposedly because he had suffered the disconcerting experience of watching his own funeral while sitting on that very same pew, surrounded by his grieving, mourning friends and family members. The name of this older gentleman is George, according to Misty, and he is said to spend much of his time in fits of tears and expressions of deep sorrow. It is interesting to note that George is a mobile spirit: he goes wherever the pews go. When they were located in the doll room, for example, he was extremely active in that area.

During an EVP session carried out in the chapel one afternoon, investigators Randy Schneider, Jen Roderick, and Sean Rice were attempting to make contact with any entities that might be present. In the corner of the room, an Ovilus device was running quietly. Within the paranormal research community, opinions on the Ovilus are fiercely divided. Advocates claim that the device does just what it claims to do, allowing discarnate entities to manipulate energy levels around it and therefore cause the device to display (or speak, if one turns the volume up) specific, carefully chosen words from an internal database or dictionary; skeptics, on the other hand, take the position that the Ovilus is at best an exercise in wishful thinking, and at worst may be a cold-hearted scam designed to separate the gullible from their money. At the time of writing, the jury is still out.

The Ovilus device said the name "Frank" twice during the same session; was this simply coincidence, or was Frank a spirit who was trying to communicate with the trio of researchers? The latter explanation is given a little more weight when one considers the fact that not too far from here, a male voice whispered the name "Frank" in Misty's ear when she was walking through the old x-ray room located just a little to the south.

The two child spirits who haunt the chapel are named Jessica and Christian, and they are by far the most active spirits within the vicinity.

x x x x x

Kimm Andersen is a passionate collector of arcane memorabilia, which he uses to enrich the look and atmosphere of Asylum 49 whenever the opportunity presents itself. Friends and family are often on the look-out for such oddities on Kimm's behalf, and so when the opportunity arose to purchase a haunted rocking horse, of all things, a long-time friend named Jen naturally jumped at the chance, and kindly gifted it to Asylum 49.

The rocking horse had an interesting backstory. It was electrically powered, and would suddenly spring to life all on its own, usually at around three o'clock in the morning. Finally, the seller's wife decided that enough was enough and she gave him an ultimatum: *You either get rid of that thing, or you get rid of me!*

He put it on eBay that same day.

Kimm brought it to the Asylum with the idea of it being a toy or distraction to keep young Jessica and Christian entertained. However, the rocking horse may have a very dark history. According to Misty, she communicated with the spirit of an adult male who was strongly attached to the toy. When the psychic asked him about the nature of that attachment, he reluctantly confessed to her that during his lifetime, he had been an abuser and molester of children, and had used the rocking horse as a lure.

"He is extremely ashamed and remorseful for his actions now," Misty explains, shaking her head sorrowfully, "but he wasn't that way in life, and he ruined the lives of a lot of innocent children."

When the spirit of this vile man began to haunt the conference room, his presence intimidated the young children who are in residence there to such an extent that Kimm finally decided to cut his losses and get rid of the rocking horse, hoping that the twisted entity would go along with it. The move appeared to be a successful one, because Jessica and Christian are active once more inside the chapel and surrounding areas.

Among the other spirits to be found inside the chapel are those of several teenagers and children, most of whom seem interested in nothing more than hanging out together and simply killing time. One is a girl with short blond hair, whose apparition glows with a bright light when she appears before surprised eyewitnesses.

During the days in which the hospital was still open for business, the conference room often served as a gathering place for its employees; it is no different during today's ghost hunts, when both novice and experienced paranormal enthusiasts flock there in order to spend a few hours attempting to communicate with the ghosts that haunt it.

There is rarely a surfeit of EVPs, K-II EMF meter activity, and flashlight responses to questions inside the chapel. EMF meters such as the TriField measure levels of electromagnetic energy in the environment. There is much speculation among members of the paranormal research community regarding a potential link between high levels of EMF and the occurrence of ghostly activity. Some believe that such energy allows spirits to manifest in our physical world.

Kids are known for having almost boundless levels of energy in life, and it would appear that it is no different once they have passed on from this life to the one beyond it, for both Jessica and Christian will frequently roll flashlights and other objects around the surface of the conference room table, sometimes pushing them off the edge and onto the floor if it suits their mood. They seem to love the attention and applause that they receive when they perform in front of a rapt and attentive audience.

Several visiting investigators have reported sightings of an extremely tall and slender gray apparition standing in the chapel doorway, and have all remarked upon its stretched, elongated arms, torso, and legs, all of which look distinctly inhuman: In fact, it calls to mind images of the fictional character "Slender Man," who has become so prominent in both the paranormal and mainstream media of late.

No detail or definition is ever seen in the figure's facial features, making it impossible to determine whether it is male or female. When asked to estimate how tall the figure was, one paranormal investigator placed it at somewhere close to seven feet tall.

When Richard Estep and fellow investigators Sean Rice and Jason Fellon had first visited Asylum 49 in the spring of 2015, they had spent a portion of the evening investigating within the chapel. Nothing of any note had taken place that night, and the three had left more than a little disappointed.

Their return visit that same Halloween would have rather more disturbing results.

During their initial walkthrough of the former hospital, first-time investigator Autumn Kingry walked past the large old pipe organ, which sits directly outside the chapel entrance, without noticing anything unusual. She did this several times during the next few days, and each time suffered no ill effects at all.

On the day that Sean and Richard were due to focus their investigation on the chapel, Autumn was making her rounds just as she had during the past few days, when she suddenly stopped dead in her tracks. She was overcome by a wave of intense emotion, the likes of which she had rarely experienced before, and then burst into tears with no apparent cause.

"All of a sudden I started crying," Autumn recounts, "I had no idea why I became so emotional, but almost as soon as it had started, it was gone again."

Asylum 49 stalwarts Cathy Blank and Cami Andersen took time out of their hectic schedules to accompany Richard and Sean for an EVP session inside the chapel. It had been a busy and stressful week for all concerned, and both men had been staying awake for long hours during their stay at the haunt; however, the atmosphere was very casual and relaxed, and what started out as a serious and somber evening of paranormal investigation soon loosened up into an informal round of storytelling and a bevy of bad jokes.

Pretty soon, laughter and lightheartedness were the order of the day, which seemed a little out of place inside the haunted chapel, where the four investigators sat amongst the ghostly figures in white that occupied every row of pews. Unusually for the chapel, their EMF meters barely flickered, with each K-II offering up at most a single desultory light every now and then, but nothing more.

The air inside the chapel was growing warm, bordering upon hot, and getting uncomfortably so, to such an extent that everybody was starting to sweat.

Discussion soon turned to the spirits of Jessica and Christian, and then to the tall, stick-thin figure that has been glimpsed standing inside the chapel doorway. Although nobody realized it at the time, Sean had stopped laughing and joking along with the others several minutes back, and fell into an uncharacteristically brooding, sullen silence. As somebody who is usually an absolute chatterbox and the first person to either crack a joke or laugh at somebody else's, this was a bizarre turn of events.

Finally noticing that something was wrong, Richard turned to Sean and asked him if he was doing okay. The response was a noncommittal grunt.

"Are you sure?"

"No." Sean's reply was clipped and terse.

"What's wrong?" Richard asked, the hackles suddenly rising on the back of his neck.

"I feel angry. Don't know why."

"Do something for me," Cathy asked, obviously concerned at Sean's out-of-character mood swing. "Stand up and come over here." Sean obeyed without question. "Now take three or four deep breaths."

Sean was instructed to sit down in a different seat, on the opposite side of the room. Once he did, he told everyone that he was starting to feel a little better. Slowly, with just a little help from Richard, the two girls began to turn Sean's mood around, cracking jokes and coaxing what were first smiles and then a few genuine laughs out of him.

Privately, Richard was worried about his friend. It simply wasn't *like* him to get angry. In fact, through all the years that he had known Sean, Richard had *never* seen him either get angry or lose his temper . . . before coming to Asylum 49.

"It's that pew," Cami explained, pointing at Sean's original seat, which was sandwiched in between two white-garbed dummies. She went on to relate how many visitors to the chapel had felt negative emotions ranging from irritation to full-blown anger and rage when sitting in that particular spot—feelings that always dissipated and then vanished entirely whenever they moved to sit elsewhere.

"I felt fine when we were walking around today," Sean explained afterward, "but when I sat down in here . . . it started as irritation, agitation, maybe, but then I got this feeling of something not being quite right."

Richard, Cami, and Cathy were supportive, nodding at Sean to continue. He looked each of them in the eye and seemed a little embarrassed to admit that just a few minutes before he had been asked to stand up, he had developed an almost overwhelming urge to scream at them all. "I wanted to yell at you all, tell you to just shut the f—up!" Sean admitted bashfully. "I don't know where it came from, exactly, but I was *this* close to doing it, just for a second.

"I have *never* felt as irritated, frustrated, or angry as I have sitting here," he went on, getting more and more puzzled as he examined his feelings from every possible angle, "and I just don't get it. It's not the heat or the conversation. I feel so much better now I've moved." He looked over at the empty pew suspiciously.

"So why don't *you* try it?" Cami suggested, looking over at Richard. She had a point. As anybody who knows them both will attest, Richard is much more likely to get angry or frustrated than Sean, being much more of a "type A" personality by nature than his placid friend.

Somewhat nervously, Richard stood up and moved across the chapel to sit in what was fast turning into the hot seat. The good-natured humor continued, with everybody keeping a watchful eye on Richard, but the Englishman had to admit that he wasn't feeling anything out of the ordinary.

"You're not irritated?" Sean asked skeptically, wiping sweat from his brow with the back of one hand. He sounded just the slightest bit disappointed.

"Nope," Richard admitted, before amending it with "well, maybe just a little . . ."

"Oh yeah, really?" The big investigator sounded more optimistic now. "Why?"

"I'm annoyed that I'm not getting angry, mate." Richard flashed him an apologetic smile. "But I'm guessing that isn't what you were going for, is it?"

Beneath all of the joking around, Richard was secretly deeply concerned about the effect that the Asylum was having on Sean. The pair had investigated countless haunted (and not so haunted) locations together, and not once had Richard witnessed his friend having any kind of emotional meltdown. Now, Sean had experienced two in the space of as many days.

Perhaps Sean's having recently lost his grandfather might be a contributing factor, Richard mused, not to mention the fact that the entire team was working long days and very late nights investigating the former hospital. They were running on a decidedly less-than-healthy diet of energy drinks and junk food, which was hardly optimal when it came to keeping their nerves calm and their minds relaxed.

Yes, Richard attempted to convince himself, maybe *that* was it: a combination of fatigue, lack of sleep, and a high caffeine intake might be behind Sean's two highly uncharacteristic mood swings. He recalled that Autumn had also been reduced to tears for no apparent reason, so perhaps the stress was beginning to show on all of them, and cracks were starting to appear in the emotional well-being of his team.

Or maybe the explanation was something even more concerning. After all, the rest of the team had kept their emotions under control without too much effort, and so had the Andersens.

Richard resolved to keep a closer eye on his teammates from here on out, just in case there was something more to this than met the eye.

9

Into the Fear Cage

During the days in which the Tooele Valley Hospital was still functioning as a healthcare facility, its employees were quite rightfully given their own staff lounge and kitchen, two rooms that can be found just off the main hallway and directly next door to one another.

Caffeine has always been the drug of choice for the healthcare provider, and without it, many a doctor, nurse, or paramedic would have fallen asleep on their feet during a long and tiring shift. Having a private sanctum that would allow them to get out of the way of the patients and families for a while, and snatch either a safety nap or, at the very least, some precious personal time, would have been invaluable to the men and women who kept the hospital running.

Nowadays, both rooms look very different indeed. A fake fireplace and wall full of leather-bound books greet the visitor when they walk inside, but the first thing that draws the eye is the life-sized *Blair Witch*-style stick figure that lies propped up against one wall, accompanied by a number of animal skulls. A flock of birds hangs lifelessly from the ceiling, obviously the work of a very skilled taxidermist, and it's easy to get the impression that they are swooping down on you in a style of which Alfred Hitchcock would most definitely approve.

Although it may not be paranormal in nature, nobody has yet been able to satisfactorily explain the sweetly cloying odor that permeates this room. One commonly held theory is that it is simply a remnant of the perfume worn by the female nurses, though that would seem unlikely after so many years when one experiences just how pungent the smell is in that room for themselves.

On a table in the center of the room lies a mannequin crafted into the form of a woman who is wearing a black and purple dress. She wears a look of horror upon her face, which is partially explained by the fact that her eyelids appear to have been surgically removed.

Brushing aside a red velvet curtain, one walks into what can quite reasonably be called a *fear cage*. This is a term that has been coined by paranormal investigators to describe rooms or areas in which electromagnetic fields (EMF) are *extremely* strong. Medical science acknowledges that long-term exposure to high levels of electromagnetic energy can cause potentially serious side effects to one's overall health, particularly within the brain. They also make the experiencer much more susceptible to becoming severely anxious and borderline paranoid. Depending upon their belief system, it is not unusual for people who are spending time in a fear cage to believe with total and utter certainty that they are in the presence of angels, demons, ghosts, fairies, aliens, or other supernatural beings.

Another intriguing possibility that is often discussed by those who investigate such matters is the theory that rather than simply inducing hallucinations in the brain, the high levels of EMF are acting as some kind of energy source, which in turn serves to fuel real paranormal activity.

One thing that can be said for certain is that the electromagnetic field levels in the former staff lounge and kitchen were very high indeed, so much so that using EMF meters as a paranormal research tool was basically a waste of time.

To make matters worse, the devious minds behind the design and layout of Asylum 49 have filled this particular fear cage with *dolls*. It really is filled, completely stacked from floor to ceiling with dolls of every conceivable shape, size, and variety; life-sized mannequins in lacy ball-gowns grin through serrated teeth at visitors from their position next to delicate porcelain dolls that are dressed as little girls. Rag dolls sit comfortably alongside the most terrifying children's toy of all, the cuddly circus clown.

Welcome to the "fear cage," a room filled to the rafters with dolls of all sizes.

Some of the dolls are sprayed a demonic-looking green color, whereas others have been carefully painted in cold white tones. No matter their differences, the dolls all have one thing in common: their cold, lifeless glass eyes, which seem to follow you around the room no matter where you choose to stand.

Standing in the middle of the doll room, it is almost impossible not to shudder when looking around and finding yourself being watched by hundreds of sets of dead, sightless eyes. Once in a while, the dolls are said to move about the room without the intervention of any living person.

For her part, Asylum 49 psychic Misty Grimstead is convinced that a number of the dolls are haunted by their own unique *attachments*—spirits that came along with the dolls from their last location, carried along to their new home as some sort of paranormal parasite.

In 2014, the mannequins that are made out of pillows and white sheets and which now reside on the benches in the chapel, used to be stored inside the doll room. During that year's Halloween haunted house, Misty played the role of a ghostly woman in black, which required secreting herself in a dark corner of that fear cage. With a shudder, she recalls seeing the heads of the mannequins turning backward and forward, all at the same time. She is adamant that there were no breezes or drafts running through the doll room that might explain the extremely creepy movements.

x x x x x

Although some investigators don't like to believe that it will ever happen to them, it is nonetheless true that if one delves into the paranormal realm for long enough, they will eventually have an entity follow them home. It is an experience that has happened to both authors of this book, and in each case it happened after they had spent time at Asylum 49.

Sometimes the roaming entity is a child, perhaps seeking the comfort and security of a mother or father-figure; sometimes it is an adult spirit, which pursues the investigator for one of a thousand possible reasons; and sometimes, on what tend to be mercifully rare but nonetheless very disturbing occasions, the unwitting investigator is followed by something that is genuinely sinister and evil.

It was a ghost hunt that was just like any other ghost hunt. Kimm had just given his usual presentation of evidence at the beginning of the evening, followed by the traditional walking tour, and the evening finally culminated in an overnight investigation of the old hospital. There were groups of people scattered all through the building, each with their own technical equipment and personal agenda. Camera flashes burst in every doorway and throughout the long corridors, lighting up the hordes of latex zombies, demons, and other nightmarish creatures that seemed to lurk in every alcove and cubby-hole.

There are two other particularly well-known spirits in residence within the staff lounge and kitchen: one is the ghost of an adult male, and the other is that of a little boy. The two always seem to manifest together.

On this particular evening, Kimm went in and sat with the group who had chosen this as their starting point. He noticed that both Cami and regular investigator Cathy Blank were in there too. The ladies already had their digital voice recorders running, and they had placed flashlights in one of the doorways.

"Will you please turn on one of those flashlights?" asked one of the visiting group members hopefully.

The group waited for a moment, looking expectantly toward the doorway that separated the staff lounge from the kitchen. The flashlights were barely visible on the floor, reflecting back very little of the moonlight that was coming in through the windows.

Suddenly, about four feet high up the doorframe, the Asylum 49 staff members watched in amazement as a little shadow figure tentatively peeked its head into the room.

"Watch the door on the right-hand side, about four feet up and you'll see the little boy is poking his head around the door and is looking at us," said Kimm to the group.

The visitors took him at his word, gasping when they caught sight of the shadowy little head. This was actually a fairly common occurrence for this particular area, but it was easily overlooked if the uninitiated visitor wasn't paying attention or didn't know what specifically to look for.

"Keep watching for shadows. Now that you've seen the little boy, you might spot the tall man that comes along with him most of the time."

"What does he look like?" one of the visitors whispered raptly.

"Look for the darkness to become even darker," Kimm answered, before turning his attention back to the figure in the doorway and raising his voice just a little. "Come into the doorway and bend down to turn the flashlight on please," he coaxed, speaking directly to the little shadow figure. "It's alright. We can see you, and I promise that we aren't going to hurt you. We'll just stay right where we are."

In total silence, the incredulous visitors and investigators watched as a child-sized shadow stepped hesitantly out into the dimly moonlit doorway, bent down, and turned the flashlight on.

The entire room held its breath. Nobody said a word; they simply watched, eyes wide, as the figure darted back around the doorframe again, going back to peeking in shyly at the room full of strangers. Finally Kimm whispered, "Thank you."

For the next half hour, the ghostly little boy turned the flashlights on and off in answer to various questions, coaxed gently by the Asylum 49 staff members and their guests. Finally, the shadow figure simply vanished, as though a switch had been suddenly turned off. The flashlights lay still and dark in the doorway, their lack of light signifying the end of what had been a truly remarkable communication session.

It was getting late, and the Asylum 49 crew was getting tired. Most of them had worked all day long, and had pushed on late into the night in order to make the ghost hunt happen. For his part, Kimm also had to get up early that following morning as well, having a lot of things to take care of at his day job, and so he decided to call it a night. As soon as the visitors had left, he locked the front doors up tight and drove straight home, thinking about nothing more than sinking into his soft, warm bed and catching a few precious hours of sleep.

When he got home, Kimm went to the bathroom before heading to bed. As he walked out of the bathroom, he turned the light switch off. Before he had even reached the side of his bed, the bathroom light flipped itself back on again.

More annoyed than afraid, he turned around and walked back to the bathroom, poking his head through the doorway and making sure of what he already knew perfectly well to be true: there was nobody inside—nobody *physical*, at least. Mumbling incoherently under his breath, Kimm turned the light off again and began to walk back to his bed.

The bathroom light turned itself on again.

Kimm now knew for sure that one of the ghosts had followed him home and he was not in the least bit amused. He was exhausted, cranky, and borderline angry; with an early start ahead of him, he had not the slightest desire to play games with a runaway Asylum 49 spirit. Stomping back to the bathroom, he reached out and flipped the light off again.

"Not tonight! Leave the damn light off and let me get some freaking sleep!"

Turning back and heading for his bed for what he hoped would be the final time tonight, Kimm suddenly stopped dead in his tracks. It sounded as though all hell was breaking loose in the bathroom, an explosion of clattering and thudding that made him wince just to hear it. He rushed back to find out just what had happened. Flipping the light back on, he saw that all of the items that had been sitting on the bathroom sink had been swept off, and now lay in a scattered jumble on the floor.

Kimm was so tired that he just rolled his eyes in the face of the paranormal temper tantrum, swore quietly under his breath, and went back to bed, reasoning that cleaning up the mess could wait until tomorrow.

Taking off his clothes, he climbed into bed and pulled the blankets up over him with a contented sigh. It wasn't long before he was on the verge of drifting off to sleep. Then he heard the disconcerting sound of footsteps approaching the bottom of his bed. Even in this semi-sleeping state, Kimm knew full well that this wasn't a break-in or any kind of physical intrusion. He rolled over to look, wanting to know just which of the Asylum's ghostly inhabitants had seen fit to accompany him home, and sure enough, he saw the shadowy figures of the tall man and the little boy from the staff lounge. Both were pacing back and forth at the foot of his bed.

Kimm was normally very tolerant of the old hospital's spirits, reasoning that they had every bit as much of a right to walk its hallways as he and the other flesh and blood people did. But coming into his home uninvited was an entirely different story. This was *his* place, not theirs, and they were now cutting into his precious sleeping time.

Kimm pointed an accusatory finger at the tall man. "*You* can't be here," he growled. "Go home!" Then, softening a little, he pointed at the little boy. "*You* can stay, but you have to sit down and be quiet."

The tall man instantly disappeared: one second he was there, and the next he simply wasn't, having dissipated in the blink of an eye. The little boy crouched down beside the foot of the bed. Kimm burrowed under the covers and went back to sleep, no longer caring who or what was there as long as he could snatch some shred of rest before the sun came up.

On the following evening, there happened to be yet another ghost tour. It wasn't particularly remarkable or eventful, and when the night was over, Kimm once again went home to get some rest. He walked into the house with nothing on his mind other than an eagerness to catch some sleep, but something felt wrong to him as soon as he had turned his key in the lock; instead of being greeted with the calm, friendly atmosphere that most of us associate with our homes, he had instead walked into an eerie, almost foreboding feeling that instantly set his nerves on edge.

The atmosphere was heavy and oppressive, though Kimm could think of no reason for it . . . except for his uninvited guests of the night before. His sense of unease only grew stronger as he went about his usual bedtime routine, and by the time he finally got into bed, he had resolved to simply brush it aside and get some sleep.

His nerves still on edge, Kimm lay in bed and tried to drift off to sleep. He felt as if he was being watched by someone standing right next to his bed. He quickly opened his eyes and jumped, startled.

There was a large shadow lurking at the bedside.

Kimm flipped the nightstand lamp on and laughed at himself for being such a wimp. The shadow he saw was nothing more than the treadmill, which had a coat draped over it. He turned the light off, and rolled over to go to sleep once again, but still couldn't quite shake the feeling of unease.

He lay there for a very long time, and finally fell asleep after what felt like hours. It felt as though Kimm hadn't been out for very long when something began to nudge him back toward wakefulness. It was a smell, a horrible stench, something akin to rotting or diseased flesh. It grew stronger and more potent as he began to fully awaken, wafting into his nostrils and coating the back of his throat as though it was an invisible, rancid pool of sludge that was so thick, Kimm could practically taste it.

Gagging and struggling to hold down the contents of his stomach, he tried to get out of bed in order to investigate the source of the stench, but was shocked to discover that he couldn't move a muscle. There was something heavy pressing down on his chest, so forcefully that he could barely take a breath. More worrying still was the fact that the more he struggled to move, the heavier the weight seemed to become, until it felt as if he was being pinned beneath a massive boulder that was slowly crushing him into the mattress.

As he lay there helplessly, fighting to breathe and to get his muscles to obey even the most simple of commands, Kimm's eyes widened in terror. A shapeless dark mass was beginning to manifest in the air above his chest, forming silently and blacking out the ceiling. Whatever this manifestation was, it was shadowy yet solid, and above all, it was malicious.

Kimm had heard of this type of thing before, from reading the paranormal literature and talking to other investigators. Such incidents rarely ended well for those involved. "I'm not going down like this!" he thought to himself desperately. Summoning up all of his willpower, in one explosively swift move Kimm shoved the bedclothes and the solid black mass off of him.

The oppressive weight was suddenly gone, allowing Kimm to finally take in a shuddering, gasping breath. Air had never tasted so sweet. Filling his lungs with it, he bolted out of bed and whirled around, ready to take on whatever evil entity had attacked him in his own home, but both the dark form and the rancid stench were gone, and everything was back to normal.

For now.

x x x x x

Kimm chose to keep the disturbing experience to himself. His mind was still processing the terrifying events of that night, and he was particularly concerned about their dark and threatening nature. Although the word "demonic" is one that is tossed around too often and easily within the circles of paranormal research, the nocturnal assault could easily fall under that particular category.

This was not the first time that Kimm had seen such a black mass, however; he (and other Asylum 49 investigators) had sighted something similar in the old staff lounge and kitchen area, usually moving around the room, or simply hovering in place. What *was* new, on the other hand, was the entity's aggressive behavior, and its apparent willingness to follow the living home.

The following weekend brought with it yet another ghost hunt. Kimm slipped easily back into his usual routing of presentation-tour-investigation, and the sinister events of the week before were mostly gone from his mind, supplanted by a week's worth of professional concerns and the business of day-to-day living.

He no longer remembers whether he chose to start out the night's investigation in the staff lounge and kitchen, or whether he was perhaps drawn there, but whichever is the case, Kimm began the evening by hunkering down in the same room in which he had helped to draw out the tall man and the young boy just a few days before.

Cami Andersen and Cathy Blank were already shepherding the visitors through their attempts to communicate with any entities that might be present in the room, using an SB-7 Spirit Box as a tool. It wasn't long before the shadow figures of the young boy and the older man obliged the investigators by showing themselves, but this time, something was very different about their behavior.

Both shadowy figures appeared to be pointing toward one of the far corners of the room, an area which was bathed deeply in shadow. The Asylum 49 staff members and their guests all turned to look, peering into that particular corner in an effort to make out whatever it was that the spirits were indicating.

It was then that Kimm realized exactly what it was: the amorphous black mass that had attacked him in the night. It was floating in mid-air at the junction of two walls, and seemed to be patiently observing the goings-on inside the staff lounge.

At various points throughout the flashlight communication session, the dark shape would move, drifting toward the two shadow figures. They, in turn, would move away, always keeping their distance from it and never letting it get within arm's length. It was as though the two spirits were afraid of the darker entity, or perhaps knew of its capacity for violent and harmful behavior.

Asylum 49 investigators had seen the black form in this room before, but never at the same time as the two more gentle spirits of the man and boy.

Suddenly the spirit box barked out: *We are not performing circus monkeys!*

Cathy and Cami respectfully apologized to the spirits for giving them a bad impression. They weren't trying to make them feel as though they were some type of side show, the ladies explained; they only wanted to communicate with them, and to find out a little more about their lives and backstories. Kimm, on the other hand, was coming to the conclusion that the message was aimed squarely at him.

Up until that moment, Kimm really *had* seen this as primarily a performance for the audience and he now began to feel more than a little guilty about that. He realized that just as in life, so it sometimes was in death: Some spirits wanted to talk and communicate with the living, whereas some just wanted to be left alone, allowed simply to mind their own business.

Several months before, Kimm had recorded an EVP in the staff lounge area that had made this very point, emphasizing that the spirits there were not performing for the amusement or entertainment of the living. Much to his subsequent regret, Kimm had blown off what he now saw as a warning: *Either treat us with respect, or be prepared to take the consequences.*

Upon further reflection, he was coming to believe that the spirits of the man and boy had followed him home for a very specific reason: They had come to warn him about the impending attack from the dark mass, whose room they shared back at the hospital. Nor was the attack purely random and malevolent, or so it now seemed to Kimm; he was convinced that it had been motivated by what some of the entities at Asylum 49 saw as his continuing, willful treatment of them as a sideshow performance, rather than appreciating them as spirits who had once been living, breathing people just like himself.

Looking upon them in a totally different light now, Kimm nicknamed the man and the young boy "The Messengers."

Today, visitors to the Asylum are given a very clear warning when they enter the staff lounge and kitchen: "In this room there are three spirits: a tall male shadow figure, a small young boy shadow figure, and a bigger black mass. The man and the boy shadow figures are fine for you to communicate with . . . but if you see the big black shadow, you continue at your own risk. He—or *it*—doesn't like to communicate with the living, and would like you to know that he is not a performing circus monkey . . ."

10

The Temporary Morgue

Rather unusually for a facility of its type, the Tooele Valley Hospital was not built with a morgue. When one considers the regularity with which patients tend to die in even the very best of hospitals, it seems like quite a short-sighted decision on the part of the hospital architects and administrators.

Their solution was a simple one: Place the bodies of the newly deceased out of sight (and therefore out of mind) in Rooms 20 and 21, which played the role of a temporary morgue prior to the bodies of the deceased being released to the coroner for further processing.

Soon after they had begun to run the very earliest ghost tours, the Asylum 49 staff was to learn the first of many valuable lessons. As time went on and the confidence of the guides grew, the tours became longer and much more detailed, interweaving the stories of the EVPs that were being caught, instances of people being touched by unseen hands, and numerous cases of visitors hearing and seeing things that seemed genuinely paranormal in nature.

Some of the tour guides spent so much time at the hospital that the spirits seemed to become somewhat comfortable with their presence there; they started opening up a little and began to share some of the most intimate details of their lives and deaths, primarily through the medium of EVPs.

One night, while conducting a private tour in Room 21, Kimm and his tour group first got themselves comfortable, and then began to conduct an EVP session, as had already been done so many times before.

He began by asking the standard questions that one almost always asks when doing an EVP session: "Is there anyone here who'd like to talk to us?" Pause. "What is your name?" Pause. "How old are you?" Pause. "Were you a patient here?" Pause. "Did you work here?" Pause. "If you were a patient, why were you at the hospital?" Pause. "If you were a patient, do you remember what happened?"

After about 20 minutes had passed, Kimm and his group left Room 21 in order to investigate elsewhere. He fully expected to have recorded some EVPs; it's rare that one doesn't get at least one EVP when experimenting at the hospital, simply because it is so paranormally active. Obtaining multiple anomalous voices on the recording is much more common, and it is a rare night indeed when nothing at all turns up during analysis.

The group reviewed the recordings during the next few days. When they got to the session from Room 21, everybody was astounded at what had been caught. They had captured nothing less than a full-blown conversation with the spirits in there!

"Is there anyone here who'd like to talk to us?"

A young boy answered. "Yes."

"What is your name?" The boy revealed his first name.

"Were you a patient here?"

"Yes."

"If you were a patient, why were you at the hospital?"

This time, two separate spirit voices answered.

"We died here," said the first.

"Caught a bullet," gabbled the second, almost too quickly to hear.

"If you were a patient," Kimm continued, "do you remember what happened?"

The young boy responded and told the group that a family member had accidentally shot him dead, and that he had died in the hospital, his body finally being placed in Room 21.

Naturally, this information made it into the tours. One night, Kimm was giving a tour as usual. When he reached the doorway of Room 21, he began telling the incredible story of the young boy who had died tragically from a gunshot wound. He then noticed that a woman in the group was crying. He continued with the tour, but made a mental note to find the woman who had been crying and make sure that all was well.

After the tour, Kimm approached the woman discreetly. "I couldn't help but notice that you were crying during the tour," he began, somewhat awkwardly. "Are you okay?"

Her body language immediately began to change, and when the lady turned to look at him, Kimm could see that she was growing increasingly angry, although he had no idea why. When she clenched her fists at her sides, however, he took an involuntary step backward and raised his hands placatingly. With tears in her eyes the lady said, "That little boy you talked about—the one who died in Room 21—he was my nephew."

Kimm started to explain, or at least tried to, but the woman simply cut him off. "How did you know about him?" she demanded, jabbing an accusatory finger at him. "You mentioned details that nobody knows—that nobody *could know*, unless they were family. So who told you? Nobody was supposed to say *anything!* We're trying to protect the person who shot him. Only a few people in the family know all those details. So who was it that told you?"

Kimm's stomach lurched at the news. He could hardly believe what was happening. A story that was so amazing to him, one that had felt like a huge breakthrough in the Asylum 49 investigations, had suddenly become bittersweet with this horrible new revelation. It hadn't been their intent to hurt or upset anybody, simply to share the information that had been passed on via the medium of EVP. Kimm was starting to get a little nervous about the ramifications of this new discovery, and wondered how best to handle the situation.

Finally, he decided that telling the truth, no matter how unbelievable it might sound, was the best policy. "Your nephew told us himself," Kimm admitted, gently lowering his voice. "I'm really so sorry that you heard it like this. I didn't mean to upset you. I had no idea that something like this was going to happen."

The woman crossed her arms defiantly, obviously still angry, and totally unconvinced that her nephew's spirit really had told Kimm about his death. She was certain that a family member must somehow have betrayed the secret and told him, and she demanded to know their identity.

"I don't want to upset you any more than I already have," Kimm said, "but if you'd like, I'll go home and get the recording so that you can hear it for yourself."

She told him to go and get the recording, challenging Kimm to prove that it was indeed her nephew speaking from beyond the grave. Kimm was completely silent during the short drive home. After snatching up the recorder, he headed straight back to the hospital with it, his mind still abuzz with a whirlwind of thoughts. Would the lady believe her own ears? Would she get even angrier still, entering a state of denial and taking her grief out on the people at Asylum 49?

There was only one way to find out. He played the recording for the woman as soon as he returned to the hospital, and watched silently as her eyes widened, and tears began to fill them once more.

She slowly put her hands over her mouth. "That's him, it's really his voice." She stopped crying suddenly and looked Kimm right in the eye. "Is he stuck here? Did he not cross over?"

Kimm had thought that this situation couldn't possibly get any worse, but it just had. He didn't know the answers to any of her questions. How could he fix this? How could he make it right?

"I don't know if he's stuck here," he admitted slowly. "I mean, I don't *feel* that he is, but I can't say for sure one way or the other."

"Can we go and ask him?" the woman instantly countered.

Oh no, Kimm thought, *this could go downhill really fast.* But he quickly realized that he had no choice in the end, when it came right down to it. He had started this, and now it was up to him to finish it. "We can go see if he's there and if he will answer us," he replied with a distinct lack of enthusiasm, hoping that this whole thing wouldn't simply blow up in his face.

They walked slowly toward Room 21 together, both of them maintaining an awkward silence, and then sat down on one of the creaky old hospital beds. The vinyl mattress crinkled and the springs squeaked as they stretched under the weight of their two occupants. Kimm reached out and gently closed the door to give them a little privacy.

The visiting woman called out the young boy's name and asked if he was there several times before they got a response. "Yes."

Kimm was overcome with relief that the boy had finally answered, validating his story. He now waited with bated breath to see whether they would get any further responses, and if they *did*, what those answers might reveal. Would they bring a sense of peace and closure to the lady, or simply serve to churn up what were already troubled waters even further?

After they verified that the boy was present, they both began to ask more questions.

"Are you stuck here?"

"No."

"Are you hurt?"

"No."

Kimm exhaled a breath that he hadn't even known he was holding. The woman was clearly getting the proof that she so desperately wanted and needed. When the night finally ended, he and the visitor were utterly exhausted after riding the emotional roller coaster that it had suddenly become. Kimm locked up the hospital securely and went home to get some much-needed sleep, relieved to have escaped from what could quite easily have become a huge disaster.

When he awoke the following morning, Kimm went straight to the computer to see if any e-mails had arrived containing EVPs from the weekend's visitors. He logged into his e-mail account and was equally horrified and fascinated to see that, yes, he had indeed gotten an e-mail. It concerned the young boy, but it wasn't from the child's aunt: It was from his *mother*, and she wanted to meet with Kimm as soon as possible. He replied straight away, requesting a convenient date and time for her to meet with him at the Asylum. After all, how could he possibly say no?

A response was not long in forthcoming. She wanted to meet him that same afternoon.

It wasn't long before Kimm was back at the hospital once more, waiting nervously for the boy's mother to get there. He greeted her warmly, and then sat down with her in the lobby to explain what exactly had happened. She listened quietly and without apparent emotion to the EVPs, patiently allowing Kimm to finish talking.

"That *does* sound like my son's voice," she said with tears suddenly running down her face. "I really want to talk to him again."

Kimm's heart ached for the woman. Her grief was clearly still all too fresh, even after the many years that had passed since his death, and yet she seemed equally eager to entertain the idea that she might have a chance to talk to him one more time. Not many of the bereaved are given that opportunity, Kimm reasoned, and who was he to deny her the chance?

"We can certainly try," he began carefully. "Please bear in mind that there's no guarantee that we will be able to contact him, though."

The woman didn't care; she just wanted to try, no matter what the odds against it may be. She was still skeptical about this truly being her son—something which must always be borne in mind, given the propensity of some spirits to imitate others. Jeremy, the Asylum's resident burn victim, is a poster child for those who like to impersonate their fellow entities. Even though it *sounded* a lot like her son, Kimm cautioned, there was a very real possibility that it wasn't him at all.

Together, the pair of them walked along the Green Mile, finally reaching the door of Room 21. Kimm had a digital voice recorder with him, and had brought a flashlight as well, intending to use it as a tool to communicate with whatever spirits might be found there.

Kimm started the recorder running and set it carefully down on a dark brown end table between the two hospital beds, and then placed the flashlight next to it.

The woman immediately began asking questions.

"Son, it's Mommy . . . are you here?"

The flashlight sprang to life instantly. She took a deep breath and continued with her questioning.

The boy's mother asked for him once again, by name this time, and the flashlight came back on instantly. For a long moment she simply sat there, unsure of what else to say, and so Kimm helped her get started.

"I want to know where you were shot," he asked gently, hoping to give the mother more proof. "If you were shot in the stomach, please turn the flashlight on now."

The flashlight stayed dark. Kimm waited several moments before continuing.

"If you were shot in the chest, please turn the flashlight on."

Again, the flashlight stayed dark. Kimm gave ample time for the flashlight to turn on, but it never did. He started asking more questions.

"If you were shot in the head, please turn the flashlight on."

The flashlight shot on and stayed on. The boy's mother burst into tears with the realization that it was indeed her son and she was talking with him once again.

After she composed herself, she asked more questions that only she and her son would possibly know the answers to; questions of a highly private and personal nature. The flashlight turned itself on and off in rapid sequence, seeming to provide answers for every question that the bereaved mother was asking. There was no hesitation whatsoever in the activity of the flashlight beam, and no confusion about the responses. They were of a definite yes-or-no nature.

Kimm was content to sit quietly, allowing his companion to drive most of the questioning. Using a series of yes-and-no questions, the mother was given more and more comforting answers. The boy told his mother to stop grieving for him, adding that he was fine and further reinforcing the fact that the shooting had been a complete accident. He wanted to make sure that the family member involved didn't get blamed for it, and that it was *supposed* to happen this way—it was, he insisted, his time to go. It was beautiful where he found himself now, and he was in possession of absolutely everything that he could ever want or need. They had been in the room for several hours by the time she finally exhausted all of her questions. She told her son that she loved him, and then the flashlight turned on for the very last time.

Afterward, Kimm escorted the woman to her car. She thanked him for making time for her, and left without saying another word. After a few weeks had passed by without his having heard anything from the woman, the whole episode slowly drifted toward the back of his mind, which was focused upon the day-to-day running of a very busy haunt. The Asylum 49 staff continued their research and investigation into the spirits who haunted the old hospital, but from then on they no longer gave out as much detail concerning the identity of those spirits in their stories.

They had had second thoughts; after all, the hospital is hardly ancient, and there were still families of people who had died there living in the surrounding area that were simply trying to go about their everyday lives. Such unexpected reminders of their lost loved ones may not be exactly welcome. These were once living, breathing people who were (and still are) both missed and deeply loved. The incident with the visitors to Room 21 was a stark reminder that, sometimes, the past can come back to haunt the present in a very literal sense.

One day, while going through his e-mail inbox, Kimm received a message from the mother of the boy who had been shot. In the e-mail, she thanked him for letting her talk to her son again. She had struggled with his passing for a long time, and said that being able to talk to him about it had given her some degree of closure and comfort. She would always love him and miss him, but said that she didn't worry for him anymore; she was no longer afflicted with visions of him suffering during his final moments, and knew for certain that nobody was to blame for his death.

The family member who had shot him was also struggling with the consequences of that horrific day, blaming themselves and wondering whether the dead boy blamed them also. It wasn't easy to carry on knowing that they had taken such a young life, which became a brutally heavy burden for them to bear, despite the knowledge that it was a complete and utter accident. Being told by the victim that it was his time to go, and that it was supposed to happen in the way that it did, had helped the person who was holding the gun immeasurably.

Kimm was greatly relieved to hear that the experience had done a great deal of good, rather than harm; his biggest fear had been that of reopening an old wound for a family that had already suffered far too much, in his estimation. He had felt absolutely terrible about having inadvertently dredged up the tragedy for the family once more, but now felt that it had happened in order to give the family some measure of solace and closure.

The staff of Asylum 49 never heard from the boy in Room 21 again, nor anything more from his family. Maybe the fleeting moment of contact had helped the boy's spirit, opening up a door of sorts that allowed him to not only get closure with his own family, but also to move on to whatever awaits us once this earthly life is over.

x x x x x

Robert Helige, Jr. (known as "Buck" to his friends) has been a security guard at Asylum 49 for many years and in that time has experienced more than his fair share of inexplicable events and bizarre encounters.

One day, the former hospital was the venue for a paranormally themed convention, known as a *paracon*. Paranormal investigators rubbed shoulders with like-minded members of the public, and Buck was having a great time meeting new people and hearing their stories. To make things a little more interesting, there was also a sprinkling of TV psychic mediums and some minor celebrities from the field of paranormal research added into the mix.

Buck and Misty were taking a stroll along the main hallway, when suddenly they heard a voice quite distinctly say the words *help me.*

The medium and the security guard exchanged a look, confirming that they had both heard the same thing. It had seemed to be coming from up ahead of them. Quickening their pace, they turned left onto the long stretch of corridor that Asylum 49 staff have nicknamed "the Green Mile."

A recliner chair that lived semi-permanently outside Room 20 now had a new occupant: an elderly lady who seemed to be in her late 80s or early 90s, with short, curly hair and a flowery night dress, stared back at them both.

"Help me," the old lady said plaintively. "He's being mean to me."

"Are you seeing this?" Buck asked out of the corner of his mouth. Misty nodded. "Can I help you, ma'am?" he asked politely.

The old lady nodded her head at him. "Yes," she said simply, and then repeated, "he's being mean."

"*Who's* being mean?" Buck wanted to know.

Suddenly, a second figure appeared to stand up behind the old lady. Whereas she was completely solid and appeared utterly real to the two eyewitnesses, this new apparition was little more than a dark approximation of a human form, far more shadow than substance. They could make out no facial features or details on him at all, in stark contrast to the frightened old lady who sat in front of him.

Buck immediately determined that whoever or *whatever* the shadowy form was, it wasn't going to be mean to the sweet little old lady, who looked like she just had to be somebody's grandma.

"Take my hand, ma'am," Buck said, politely offering her an arm. The old lady accepted it gratefully, using it as an anchor with which to get slowly to her feet. Buck felt her weight upon his arm, and yet somehow knew that it was no living being who now clutched gratefully at him for support.

With Misty trailing behind them, Buck allowed her to lead him the few short steps toward the door of Room 20. The shadowy figure disappeared into the deeper darkness of the Green Mile; whether it was the spirit of an orderly who felt that its work here was now done, or something rather less savory that was backing down in the face of the flesh-and-blood security guard, is something that remains unclear to Buck to this very day.

"Instead of just letting go, she sort of . . . like, slipped her hand *through* mine," Buck said during a recent interview. "It was the coolest thing ever. Now, whenever I go back to the hospital, I go to see if she's there."

Buck has only seen her apparition twice more since that very first encounter, but he is happy to relate that there is a big difference in her demeanor now. She no longer asks for help, and now appears to be contented and relaxed, simply watching the world go from the comfort of her recliner.

Relating the story of his encounter with the old lady's ghost to a visiting batch of paranormal investigators, Buck was delighted to learn a few days later that an EVP had been picked up on one of their digital voice records, which seemed to offer a direct response to his tale. A female voice could quite clearly be heard to say: *Yeah, he helped me.*

Buck went about his rounds with an extra spring in his step after that, particularly in the area around Room 20. If the sweet old lady ever needed his help again, he would be only too happy to oblige.

11

Cardiac Arrest

The hospital has a pair of large Emergency Rooms, which are referred to as ER #1 and ER #2, plus a pair of smaller assessment rooms known as ER #3 and ER #4. The two larger Emergency Rooms are where the truly sick and injured patients would have been brought by the EMTs and paramedics—patients with life-threatening conditions as diverse as gunshot wounds, heart attacks, respiratory arrest, and hemorrhagic shock, to name but a few.

In hospitals throughout the world, the Emergency Room is where teams of skilled medical professionals fight tooth and nail to save the lives of those who are at death's door.

Sightings of the ghostly ER doctor were getting more and more common, but each year, they always seemed to peak around the end of October. It isn't hard to understand why. After all, more ghostly activity is reported in the days and weeks running up to Halloween than at any other time of the year. That's when the nights are starting to draw in, getting colder and darker, and our minds begin to focus on the ghost stories that start to appear more frequently in the newspapers and Websites as October 31st approaches.

"That scary doctor creeped me the heck out when he popped up in the ER," is a comment that the Andersens have heard more and more often of late. Depending upon their mood, sometimes Kimm or Cami will just smile sweetly and thank the customer for their compliment; whereas at other times, they will very frankly admit that there *is* no ER doctor on their staff of performers.

Whoever—or *whatever*—they saw in the Emergency Room was not of this world.

The best working theory seems to be that this is the apparition of a doctor who used to work in the Emergency Room during his lifetime. Much of the equipment he would have used is still there. The original ER beds are also still found there, and one is forced to wonder exactly how many people breathed their last gasp on each one of them, as the staff of the Tooele Valley Hospital struggled desperately to save their lives.

Potentially, that could be hundreds, if not *thousands* of people.

Cami had seen the doctor's apparition one cold evening when she was waiting for a tour group to arrive. Leaning against a wall directly outside the Emergency Room doors, she idly scrolled through her Facebook feed while she waited.

Suddenly, something caught her eye from within the dark recesses of the ER.

The man standing beside the hospital bed was of medium height. He wore a white doctor's coat, a surgical cap, and a protective face mask. Only his eyes were visible; they stared at the empty bed, as though assessing a patient there that nobody but he could see.

Cami held her breath, sure that if she moved a muscle or even breathed too loudly, she would draw his attention. As though reading her mind, he suddenly looked up at her from out of the shadows, seeming to regard her without any emotion at all, and then vanished before her eyes.

A number of Asylum regulars have described seeing exactly the same figure, always in the same location within the Emergency Room. Consider the story of Shelby, a volunteer whose role was to lie on the ER bed and scream for help at the passers-by while a demonic doctor tormented her.

Being particularly tired that night, Shelby closed her eyes to grab a quick nap between groups of customers. Opening them again after a few moments, she was incredulous to find the doctor's apparition standing next to her bed, staring down at her from above as though sizing her up as a potential patient.

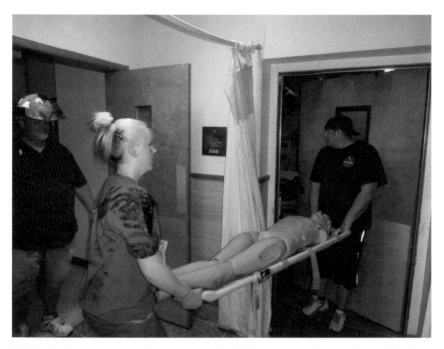

While Randy operates the helmet-cam, "EMTs" Autumn and Sean deliver their first simulated patient to the ER.

Shelby's description of the man matched Cami's precisely, and both of their descriptions tracked with that of the numerous other staff and visitors to have encountered this restless physician's ghost within the old Emergency Room.

The sheer number of visitors passing through the haunted hallways and rooms of Asylum 49 during the Halloween season seems to charge the atmosphere, giving energy for the resident spirits to play with. There can be no doubt that this is the time of year in which the ghostly manifestations are both most frequent and most active.

After the Asylum had closed for the night, Richard and his investigators carefully sealed the building off from the outside world, locking all of the doors and windows, and placing duct tape over some of the gaps in the frames in order to keep out the worst of the cold October winds.

When they were satisfied that everything was as secure as they could reasonably make it, the small team—which included a number of paramedics and nurses who had driven out from Colorado for just this purpose—set about conducting a remarkable experiment.

The body that they wheeled in on a gurney was human-shaped, but wouldn't fool even the most casual observer into thinking that it was alive. It was a rubber mannequin, designed for the sole purpose of teaching medical procedures to student EMTs, nurses, and doctors. As such, it had a very realistic airway, complete with vocal chords and a windpipe into which breathing tubes could be inserted; and rubber veins which were designed to be poked with needles and into which drugs and saline could be pushed. Attachment points on the chest even allowed the mannequin to be defibrillated, with real electric shocks administered from a cardiac monitor.

The intent of the experiment was very simple: Would a cardiac arrest in the emergency room stimulate the spirits to come forward and manifest? Could the medics coax the ghostly doctor or one of his assistants to put in an appearance during the heat of the simulated medical crisis, perhaps to lend a helping hand, as he must have done so often during his lifetime?

Although he spends much of his free time investigating claims of the paranormal and writing about them, Richard Estep is also an experienced paramedic who earns his living as a chief officer for one of America's largest private ambulance organizations.

Jennifer Roderick is also a chief officer for a private ambulance company, responsible for overseeing the clinical care for hundreds of EMTs and paramedics; Robbin Daidone is a registered nurse, whose experience includes many hours spent working in emergency rooms just like that at the old Tooele Hospital; between them, these two ladies brought the skills necessary to help run a simulated cardiac arrest in the very same bed where so many genuine emergencies had been dealt with through the past few decades.

While the paranormal investigators had spent the past hour wiring the Emergency Room up with every type of monitor and camera in their considerable arsenal, Estep had given the medical crew some very specific orders.

"I want you to make sure that emotions run high," Richard had told them firmly. "Whatever you do, and however well you do it, I'm going to make the 'patient' crash and die. If that frustrates you, if it makes you angry, then please feel free to vent those feelings right here in the room; in fact, the more emotion the better. Does that work for everyone?"

The medics had nodded their heads solemnly. For the next 30 minutes, this group of firm friends was going to make every effort to anger one another as much as humanly possible.

x x x x x

As soon as their "patient" crashed through the double doors to the Emergency Room, carried on a bright yellow plastic backboard by stand-in "EMTs" Sean Rice and Autumn Kingry, the crew was true to their word. The tension ratcheted up almost immediately, which was helped considerably by the presence of a full-body zombie female mannequin laying in the next bed, her knees spread in the childbirth position—and with a zombie baby hungrily clawing its way out of her body.

Jen stepped in to give an arrival report on behalf of the play-acting EMTs, neither of whom had ever had to give one in real life. The arrival report can be a terrifying thing for a newer emergency medical provider to have to give; it requires that they deliver a lot of information in a very small amount of time, giving bullet points in a fast, sometimes staccato-like way in front of a room full of people. It is not for nothing that resuscitation bays in Emergency Rooms are referred to as "the big room." Giving the arrival report can be a lonely experience sometimes, knowing that all eyes are on you and are quietly judging you. The Tooele Valley Hospital's ER would have seen thousands of such reports delivered over the bodies of critical patients during the course of its lifetime.

"So what we have here is a 65-year-old male," Jen began in a loud, confident voice, "with a chief complaint of dizziness and near-syncope." (*Near-syncope* means that the patient had almost fainted.) "On arrival, we could not find a heartbeat and the patient had no blood pressure."

The mannequin's sole arm hung limply over the side of the backboard, dangling like that of a dead man. Autumn and Sean had placed the backboard down on top of the hospital bed, and intentionally let the patient's dangling arm end up sandwiched between the board and the bed. Were this for real, 200 pounds of body weight would be pushing down on top of the limb, cutting off its blood supply.

"Seriously . . . you put him down on his own arm?" Richard asked, disgust very apparent in his tone of voice. Lifting the board and freeing the arm, he locked eyes with Robbin and growled, "Let *me* just take care of that." The implication of this was obvious. Richard was making it clear that, as the "doctor," he was far above such mundane matters as helping position the patient properly on the bed.

"As we were pulling into the ER bay, the patient became unresponsive with a GCS of zero," Jen went on. The GCS, or *Glasgow Coma Score,* is a measure of a patient's level of consciousness. As you sit reading this book right now, you probably have a GCS of 15, which is the highest possible. The *lowest* GCS possible is a three. To put that in perspective, even a dead body has a GCS of three. It is physically impossible to get a score of zero. Jen knew this full well, and was deliberately setting the bar for incompetence pretty high from the outset.

"GCS of *zero?*" Richard prompted skeptically.

"Yeah," Jen charged ahead, undeterred. "Unconscious. Unresponsive. Couldn't find a carotid pulse."

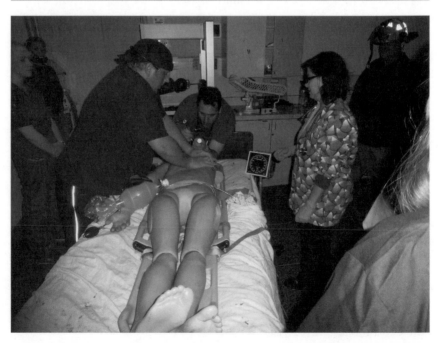

Sean performs chest compressions while Richard tries to intubate the "patient."

"Wow. The lowest GCS you can get is *three*." Richard paced around the body for a moment, carefully avoiding the hanging body of a blood-soaked nurse in the corner of the room, and then said, "Alright, so you couldn't find a carotid pulse, huh?" Obviously not trusting the EMTs, he jammed two fingers into the side of the patient's neck, searching for a pulse himself.

"No carotid pulse upon arrival," Jen confirmed.

"He's got a carotid pulse," Richard countered. "It's really slow."

This was another strike against the EMTs and was not shaping up well.

It was about to get worse, thanks to Robbin, who reached in on the opposite side of the patient's neck with her fingers to check for a carotid pulse. With Richard compressing the neck at the same time, they were basically cutting off the blood supply to the patient's brain—a fact which Robbin had deliberately calculated would make him even angrier. Sure enough, Richard drew it to her attention in no uncertain terms. His manner was getting more obnoxious with every passing mistake the team made.

Richard announced his intention to drop in an oropharyngeal airway (OPA), reaching for a small piece of curved plastic that is used to keep the tongue from falling back into the throat and blocking the windpipe. Jen asked him if he was *sure* he wanted to do that—or, she added snarkily, would he like to actually *manage* the airway.

"Which one of us went to medical school?" he fired back, telling her that he'd had quite enough of her attitude. Richard was playing the arrogant doctor role to the max, which was turning out to be rather hard work. He had nothing but respect for his fellow medical professionals, and it went against his every professional instinct to treat them so badly, but that was the entire point of the experiment.

Wiping sweat from his brow, he took a surreptitious look around the room, every square inch of which was crammed with observers and electronic monitoring equipment. He couldn't help but wonder whether his actions were being watched by unseen eyes, perhaps the spirit of the doctor said to haunt this part of the hospital, or those of former staff members or patients who had breathed their last breath in here. What would *they* make of this performance?

As he stuffed the plastic OPA into the patient's mouth, Robbin finished taking the patient's blood pressure and announced the worryingly low result to the entire room.

Richard asked for an IV to be started immediately. He had adopted the swagger and growling demeanor of the very worst kind of doctor—the martinet, one used to snapping his fingers and having their every demand catered to, instantly and without question.

Tearing a sharp needle from inside its plastic packaging, Robbin began fishing around in the patient's arm, trying to find a "vein" (actually rubber tubing) in order to start the IV. She was too professional to do anything other than mutter under her breath about what an absolute *ass* "Doctor" Estep was being.

"IV's in place," she said, sliding the plastic catheter into the rubber vein and withdrawing the needle. She dropped the needle into a red plastic biohazard container on a nearby shelf.

Puncture, remarked the Ovilus. Now that *was* interesting—the correct medical term for what she had just done wasn't "starting an IV," it was *venipuncture.*

Was it a coincidence? You be the judge.

Jen hooked the patient up to a Lifepak cardiac monitor, a state-of-the-art lifesaving device that costs thousands of dollars. Thanks to the simulation box that was running through the mannequin, a fake cardiac rhythm was being electrically generated—a very slow, very sickly heartbeat indeed, as might be seen in a patient on the brink of death.

Richard asked what rhythm the patient was in, to which Jen responded cattily, "I don't know—*you* went to med school!" Richard's own arrogant words had come back to bite him already. Rudely, he snatched the EKG printout from Jen's hand. The atmosphere in the room was growing increasingly tense, worsening with every passing barb from doctor to nurse and back again. It was perfect, *exactly* the kind of atmosphere that the investigators had been trying to create.

Power, said the Ovilus at this point, just as the Lifepak was reading the patient's dysrhythmia. One of the ways of treating a dangerously slow heartbeat is to pass electrical power through the chest in a procedure called *transcutaneous pacing.* Looking at the Ovilus log afterward, this was either a real coincidence, or perhaps a suggestion that we ought to have been treating the patient more aggressively—as indeed we should.

It was time to take things to the next level, Richard decided, as he went back to the patient's head and checked for a pulse again. He announced to the room that he couldn't find a pulse now, and asked for somebody to double-check. He exchanged a knowing glance with Jen, who took the hint right away and set the cardiac rhythm simulator to something entirely more lethal. It now looked exactly as though the patient was in ventricular fibrillation, a form of cardiac arrest where the heart was not pumping blood, but was instead quivering like a sack full of squirming maggots rather than beating cleanly as it was supposed to.

"Oh crap crap crap crap *crap!*" Richard cursed. "I guess we should . . . defibrillate?" He looked up at a room full of blank stares. Feigning hesitation, he instructed Jen to defibrillate the patient at 50 joules—*much* lower than the recommended energy level. Wordlessly, she moved to obey. Robbin and Richard began to argue about the IV line that he had asked for; seeing her opportunity to add to the chaos, Jen began talking over them both, while also charging up the defibrillator. The low whine of the Lifepak spinning up its electrical circuits filled the room, and then changed to an electronic chirping, which signaled that it was ready to shock the patient.

Telling everybody to clear the patient, Jen hit the red button and held it down until 50 joules of energy was slammed into the simulator box. Richard ordered Autumn to begin CPR, which she did with about as much enthusiasm as most people have when walking to the dentist's office for a root canal.

"It's not Hollywood CPR, *darling*," Richard snarled, emphasizing the insult. "FASTER! DEEPER! Like you *mean it!*" The mannequin began to bounce up and down on the bed as Autumn picked up the pace. She bit back the insult that was already forming, and just focused on the compressions. Her mood wasn't helped much when Robbin, acting in direct contradiction to Richard's instruction, told her to take it easy on the compressions because she was trying to work on the IV line.

"Well, *that* got worse." Richard was referring to the rhythm on the cardiac monitor, which now showed a very discouraging flat line. The patient's heart was no longer electrically active at all. He was, as they like to say in movies, "flatlining." "Give him a milligram of epi." A shot of adrenaline (also known as epinephrine) into the IV was the next move, in an attempt to generate some extra blood pressure by constricting the blood vessels and also, perhaps, kick-start the heart again.

Until now, Sean had been standing in a corner of the room, not doing much of anything except getting in the way—which was perfect. Now, Richard told him to take over CPR from "Princess" (as he had started referring to Autumn) and instructed Autumn to place a breathing tube in the patient's airway.

Big and beefy, Sean is built like a pickup truck, and he proceeded to slam the mannequin's breastbone up and down until it looked like he might actually break its spine.

Richard wanted to know how the epinephrine shot was coming along. Robbin feigned ignorance, lying, and telling him that she hadn't heard him ask for it. With all the charm of a five-year-old throwing a tantrum, Richard demanded that she get the epinephrine on board *yesterday!*

Just as the team had planned, everything was starting to go wrong. It was almost as if the Keystone Kops were running the resuscitation, and tempers were starting to fray accordingly.

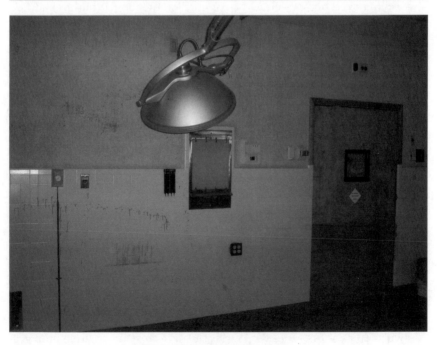

Photo of Emergency Room #1.

Despite her mother being a paramedic, Autumn did not know how to intubate the patient. After fumbling with the equipment for a moment, trying to work out which way to insert the laryngoscope blade into the patient's mouth, she finally admitted sheepishly that she didn't know how to do it. Richard yelled at her to get out of the way, demanding that Jennifer take over. Taking the equipment from her daughter, Jen bent over the mannequin's airway and began to expertly fish around with her blade, sweeping the tongue aside and pushing the breathing tube into position inside its windpipe.

Mouth, said the Ovilus while Jen was working inside the patient's mouth, trying unsuccessfully to intubate him.

There was a problem: Wanting to ratchet up the tension even further, Richard took the stethoscope from around his neck and listened to the patient's belly while air was pushed into the breathing tube using a bag.

"Gurgling," he snapped. "It's a belly tube. Pull it."

He was telling Jen that the tube was in the wrong place and that, therefore, the patient was going to suffocate. In reality, the tube was exactly where it should have been, and both of them knew it; Richard's arrogant insistence that she had placed a belly tube was calculated to cause even greater friction between them.

"Are you sure?" Jen asked, fighting to keep a lid on her temper. "Because—"

"I'm not pissing around!" Richard screamed in her face. "*Pull it!* PULL THAT TUBE!"

"Here you go, Doc—*you* do it!" She slammed the tube and bag down on the patient's face and stormed away.

Tragic, commented the Ovilus.

Robbin announced that the epinephrine was in. Nodding curtly, Richard demanded a milligram of atropine. This is a drug that we no longer use in modern-day cardiac arrests, but it would have been used very frequently when the Tooele Valley Hospital was still up and running.

Richard tried to place a second breathing tube in the patient, and then pretended to lose his temper yet again when he couldn't get the tube into the correct part of the airway. He looked up and saw a new problem displayed on the cardiac monitor. The heart rhythm that appeared on the screen needed to be shocked, and he demanded to know why it wasn't being shocked. Before she could answer, he rudely told Robbin to get out of the way so that he could do it himself.

Telling everybody to stand clear of the patient, Richard charged and shocked at 100 joules this time (which was still unacceptably low) and ordered Sean to begin CPR again. Jen stepped in instead, arguing that Sean was tired. When Richard told her that she was perilously close to insubordination, Jen told him in no uncertain terms that they could talk about it *after he was done killing this patient.*

Looking up at the IV bag hanging from the ceiling, Richard saw that the saline inside it wasn't flowing. They hadn't been giving the patient any fluid at all through the IV, thanks to the deliberately incompetent setup performed by the nurse.

Robbin and Richard began to argue about drugs. She had pushed a medication that he insisted he had never asked for. He snatched the IV out of Robbin's hands and began to work on it himself, in the process squirting a jet of salty water over the resuscitation team. *Water* was the comment from the Ovilus, which was followed less than a minute later by the word *pulse.*

In a real Emergency Room, he would probably have gotten slapped at this point. Richard was treating those who worked for him like absolute dirt. Even though it was by prior agreement with them, he felt absolutely horrible—but everybody recognized that his totally unacceptable behavior was being done as an attempt to stimulate whatever energies might be present in the area around the Emergency Rooms.

Jerk, said the Ovilus, a sentiment that nobody in the room would have disagreed with at that point.

Tempers continued to flare as nerves continued to fray. With each new mistake, Richard grew more and more belligerent and pompous, at one point insulting Sean the EMT with the title of "ambulance driver." More IVs were missed. CPR was fumbled. The simulated patient's condition continued to deteriorate. More drugs were pushed, all to no avail.

Chest, said the Ovilus, following it two minutes later with the words *cycle* (CPR is done in cycles of 30 compressions to two breaths) and *bled.*

Finally, Richard was ready to admit defeat. Obtaining the time from one of his colleagues, he pronounced the patient dead at 03:48 and printed off a final, damning EKG strip. It was a flatline.

Mistake, said the Ovilus, before repeating the word *chest.* The last word of the cardiac arrest would also go to the Ovilus. Shortly after Richard had declared the time of death, it came up with the word *certain.*

Throwing the stethoscope down, Richard stormed out of the Emergency Room like a prima donna throwing a hissy fit, slamming the door shut behind him and bringing down the curtain on the final act of the evening's drama—or so he thought.

The spirits of Asylum 49 still had their own final statement to make.

x x x x x

After a short break, Richard came back into the Emergency Room and smiled sheepishly at his crew.

"Sorry, everybody!" he apologized, and genuinely meant it.

"No you're not!" smirked Jen.

"I've noticed that your British accent gets thicker and thicker as you get angrier," Robbin laughed.

The crew cleaned everything up together, and talked about how they would run their next experiment. Nothing paranormal seemed to have occurred in the room during their pitiful excuse for cardiac arrest management, which they found frankly surprising. They quickly determined that a 15-minute break was in order, and then they would run a perfect version of the cardiac arrest simulation in the next-door ER resuscitation room. This one would be run with Jen acting in the role of the attending physician, and would go smoothly and by the book.

"After all," Richard pointed out, "you tend to catch more flies with honey . . ." Maybe the ghostly doctor (or whoever else might be present that night) would react more tangibly to professionalism than gross incompetence.

Realizing that he had left his radio in the security center, Richard told the rest of his team that he was going to get it and would be back in just a few minutes. They continued to break down the array of IV tubes, syringes, and empty drug containers that had been pushed and pumped into the mannequin's body, then began to haul it all next door to set up for the next experiment.

Arriving in the security center, Richard picked up his radio and an energy drink, and then took a minute to look at the bank of camera monitors. He stifled a yawn. Nothing much was happening on any of the screens; the Asylum was dark and quiet, with most of the lights turned out exactly as the investigators had left them.

Heading back along the main corridor, he had just passed the chapel and was beginning to think ahead to the next cardiac arrest simulation. From just up ahead and to the left, he could hear his colleagues laughing at some joke or other.

WHAM!

For a seasoned paranormal investigator of some 20 years' standing, Richard did a frankly pitiful job of keeping his cool when the heavy wooden door that he had just walked through suddenly slammed violently behind him.

This wasn't just a gentle closing. The door truly *slammed* shut, and it had waited until Richard had just cleared it before doing so. Had it happened just one second earlier, Richard realized with a growing sense of disquiet, he would have gotten a very solid door smashed directly into his face.

"Guys . . ." he looked around, circling on the spot and pulling out his flashlight, but it was obvious that there was nobody but him standing in the corridor—nobody *living*, at least.

Having heard both the slam and Richard's rather agitated tone of voice, the investigators came rushing out to join him. Despite the fact his heart pounded so hard in his chest that he felt like it might burst at any moment, Richard took several deep breaths in an attempt to calm himself, and then made sure to take a head-count as his entire team converged on his position. Each and every one of them was accounted for, which meant that unless somebody had broken into the hospital somehow (and subsequent checks revealed that all of the entrances were still locked and secured), there was practically no possibility of the slam being the work of a prankster.

Explaining exactly what had happened, Richard and the team backtracked a few steps along the hallway to the door in question.

"They always wedge these doors open during the haunted house season," Richard remembered. "So where's the wedge?"

It was lying on the carpet some four feet away from the door, a sturdy wooden chock that was used throughout the building to prevent such doors from accidentally closing in the faces of the customers and perform-ers alike, many of whom would come charging through the doorways at

Photo of a hospital bed in ER #1.

high speed, fleeing from the demonic-looking actors or chasing down their prey. The triangle of wood had been somehow removed from beneath the door, where it had been wedged quite snugly for more than a month, and the door had chosen *that precise moment* when Richard had passed through it to slam shut behind him, so close that he had actually felt the vibration against his back.

Richard began to run through the gamut of non-paranormal explanations in his mind, discussing them with his fellow investigators in an attempt to debunk what he feared was a direct personal attack.

Perhaps he had accidentally nudged it with his foot? No, that unlikely possibility could be easily discounted. Kicking a door or the wedge underneath it wasn't something you just failed to notice. Maybe it had worked itself loose in place, perhaps due to the constant tread of feet along this heavily-trafficked corridor, and had just sort of . . . slipped out. *Yes, slipped out*—for four or five feet. Again, what were the odds of that happening?

Richard hadn't made any kind of contact with the door, its frame, or the wedge holding it open. He would be prepared to swear that on the memory of his dead mother, which he actually *did* a few moments later.

"Is some doctor pissed at you?" Robbin wanted to know, voicing what Richard himself was feeling. "Is some doctor mad at the way you handled stuff back there?" She nodded in the direction of the Emergency Room.

That was *exactly* what Richard was starting to believe, and the reason why he was beginning to get more than a little jittery. He had been in hundreds of supposedly haunted places during the past 20 years, and had experienced things that most people would consider very frightening. But something about *this* particular incident was beginning to get to him, and Robbin had articulated the reason perfectly. This felt personally directed at him. Some entity—one that he couldn't see or touch—seemed to have taken offence at his boorish behavior in the ER and was making its anger known in the plainest possible terms.

For the first time in his investigative career, Richard felt singled out and targeted; it was far from a pleasant experience.

Jen took him aside for a quiet word. As Richard's boss in the paramedic service, she had seen him working under pressure before, sometimes in life-or-death situations, but had *never* seen him shaken up like this. She pointed out that his hands were trembling a little and his skin tone was even more deathly pale than his standard British color.

"I'm happy enough to run this second arrest if you want," she said, keeping her voice low and conspiratorial. "But frankly, I think you got on the bad side of something with that last one. You could probably use a little redemption in somebody's eyes, if you know what I mean."

He thought about it for a second, but didn't need much in the way of convincing to take Jen up on her offer. Maybe it was the spirit of the rule-bound doctor that had been seen in the ER, the "it's my way or the highway"-oriented physician who liked things to be done just so; maybe it was a nurse, such as the entity named Maria who acts as a sort of spiritual traffic cop along the length of the Green Mile, who had taken umbrage at Richard's border-line abusive treatment of his ER staff, including a fellow nurse.

Perhaps it was neither, and was in fact one of the Asylum's other roving spirits, cashing in on the opportunity to scoop up some free emotional energy and then spend it in scaring the heck out of an unwelcome visitor when he was most isolated from the rest of his team. Or perhaps it was something else entirely, such as the most evil and malevolent entity in the entire hospital: the Guardian.

Richard shuddered. Whatever it was, he didn't want to be in its crosshairs for even a second longer than was absolutely necessary.

"Come on," he said, faking a smile that he most definitely did not feel. "Let's go and save a life."

The second cardiac arrest did indeed go perfectly. The neighboring ER where it took place was better lit, though the blood-splatter on every visible surface and the naked legs and torso nailed upside down to the wall made it a less than comfortable environment to work in. Nevertheless, this time the IVs and breathing tubes went in first time and stayed in, and the drugs were pushed in the proper dosages at the correct times.

The atmosphere between the first and second cardiac arrests was as different as that of night from day: what they had begun to call the "Keystone Kops" debacle was a simmering tinderbox of barely suppressed anger and bitterness, whereas this time everybody was polite, calm, and respectful of one another from start to finish. There wasn't a single raised voice.

Despite the best efforts of the resuscitation team, the patient still "died." Despite what you may have seen on TV, the vast majority of those people who go into cardiac arrest outside of the hospital environment are never saved, no matter how good the first responders and Emergency Room staff are at their jobs. Pulling a sheet over the mannequin's body in silent acknowledgment of their defeat, Richard and his team paused in respectful silence after the pronouncement, before going on to break down their equipment for the night. It would soon be sunrise, and for the first time ever Richard could not wait to get out of the old Tooele Valley Hospital.

Before locking the doors and leaving for the night, the investigators paused to form a circle and then began to address any spirits of patients or medical professionals that might be present. Richard stepped up first to offer a sincere and heartfelt apology for his behavior, asking for forgiveness and promising that no harm or disrespect had been intended by the simulations in the ER that night. They honored and respected the work of the men and women who had spent years, and in some cases decades, caring for the sick

and injured of Tooele; indeed, several of those present were medical professionals themselves, and had dedicated their own lives to the same cause.

A noticeable change had befallen the atmosphere since the first cardiac
arrest. It was almost as though a safety valve had opened, relieving the pent-
up pressure that had built up around the time of the door-slamming incident.
When the last investigator left the building and closed the doors behind her,
everybody agreed that Asylum 49 felt calm and peaceful once again.

Until the next night.

12

Walking the Mile

In Stephen King's book and movie of the same name, the long walk that the condemned prisoner would take in order to be executed in the electric chair was referred to as *The Green Mile*, because the floor was the color of faded limes.

Somebody at Asylum 49 has to be a fan of the great writer, because the haunted house has its own Green Mile—except that rather than ending in a fatal date with "Old Sparky," the long stretch of green-carpeted corridor ends at a set of stout wooden doors that are kept permanently locked, for that particular doorway is the physical boundary at which Asylum 49 ends and the nursing facility to which it is connected begins.

Green camo netting hangs from the walls on either side of the corridor, not to mention covering the ceiling above your head, when you walk the Mile. To your left are the doorways that lead to the makeshift morgue Rooms 20 and 21, and on the right is the territory of the dark and malevolent entity that the Asylum 49 staff have nicknamed "the Guardian."

It is commonly accepted amongst them that the hospital has a very malevolent and sinister aspect to it, and that much of the negative energy seems to be focused and concentrated in the south wing. The Green Mile serves as a sort of informal line of demarcation, separating the lighter spirits that tend to congregate on the north side from the darker ones that prowl the south.

"I don't like to come any further than this when I'm on my own," Misty Grimstead admits, waving a hand toward the south side of the corridor and turning her head to avoid looking that way.

Several visiting psychic mediums have made the claim that a spirit vortex can also be found on the Green Mile, roughly 10 feet back from the double doors. Such vortexes are supposed to be a means of transition for discarnate entities to move from our material world into the realm of spirit. Those people who are sensitive to such things often report feeling weak, dizzy, and light-headed when passing through the area surrounding the vortex. Although there is nothing to be seen with the naked eye, psychic after psychic reports experiencing the same symptoms.

Visiting investigator Jen Roderick, who makes absolutely no claim to having mediumistic abilities, pinpointed the spot's exact location when walking the Green Mile for the first time, although other members of the team felt nothing.

The vortex is said to be guarded by the ever-vigilant spirit of a nurse named Maria, who stands at the far end of the Green Mile and acts as a sort of inter-dimensional gate-keeper. Maria was an employee of the hospital during her lifetime and remains here after her death as a guide for spirits who may be lost or confused. Some she allows to pass through into the vortex, whereas others are refused entry or redirected onto a different path.

Ever sensitive and politically correct, Kimm has nicknamed Maria "Nurse Ratched," after the infamously stiff character from the movie *One Flew Over The Cuckoo's Nest*. The moniker does seem to fit rather well, as Maria has a stern side, and is more than willing to register her disapproval when she feels the urge to do so.

To the right, on the south side of the corridor, can be found what looks to be the archetypal cabin in the woods. One half-expects the Deadite creatures from the movie *Evil Dead* to charge out at them from the doorway of the log cabin, or to be chased by a hockey-masked maniac wielding a chainsaw—either of which might actually happen one day to future visitors, if the creative staff get their way!

Photo of the nurse costumes that were used when Cami saw the ghostly nurse.
Taken in front of the maternity hall on the left and main hall on the right.

The log cabin is in fact just a façade, built up over what was once the x-ray laboratory for the hospital; much of the original x-ray equipment still survives (though it no longer functions) and is slowly gathering dust in Room 21.

During their walk-around guided tour of the hospital shortly after they first arrived, Richard Estep and his fellow investigators were led into the x-ray room by Misty. Admittedly, the lights were turned out entirely in there, rendering it pitch black, but the team became almost immediately aware of the sound of footsteps from further into the darkness and the sound of hushed, muffled voices.

"I've had my hair pulled back here, and my earrings played with," Misty states matter-of-factly, turning on a flashlight. "I've also had my butt grabbed in this room. The Guardian likes to be up here sometimes . . . not as much as he likes the maze area, but still pretty often."

"The Guardian" is the name that has been given by the staff of Asylum 49 to its darkest, most aggressive inhabitant. This malevolent entity tended to confine itself primarily to the several maze areas, but was sometimes known to come as far forward as the outskirts of the Green Mile.

The Coloradan investigators all exchanged glances, trying not to look overly concerned. Could this evil spirit be watching them from the darkness at the edge of the flashlight's beam even now?

When visitors to the haunt attraction come through the x-ray lab, actors are always lurking in the darkness, ready to give them the fright of their lives. One evening, Misty was hiding in a recessed area behind some plants, preparing to terrify the next unsuspecting victim that came her way. All was going well until she suddenly felt the sensation of fingertips running their way slowly up the side of her face. Biting her lip, she looked all around her in the darkness, but could already tell that there was nobody there—at least, nobody flesh and blood.

Misty was suddenly overcome by an overwhelming urge to run, and was helped on her way by a deep male voice rasping in her ear: "GET. OUT!"

Summoning up every last scrap of courage that she possessed, Misty walked deliberately forward, groping blindly in the darkness, until she found a group of customers that she could latch onto, and followed them out to the exit.

x x x x x

Not far from the Green Mile is an area that was originally used as the former hospital's respiratory clinic. Every day, doctors, nurses, and respiratory therapists administered nebulized breathing treatments to those patients who had been diagnosed with pulmonary disorders such as asthma, chronic bronchitis, and emphysema, to name just three.

It now serves a very different purpose indeed: It is used to store props and bits of furniture for the haunt. But it wasn't always this way; in between its time as a respiratory center and place of junk storage, this fairly large room was integrated into the haunted house itself, and saw a steady flow of customers coming through its doors on their way to the mazes. It has its own built-in restroom, which was handy for the performers who had to stand in there for hours at a time, and when it was last a part of the haunted house, the set designers had partitioned it into two distinct rooms by running a false wall down the center.

Inspired by the video game and movie franchise *Silent Hill*, the room was full of eerie faceless nurses who were liberally splattered in blood and viscera. Whereas most of the nurses were mannequins, some were actually the Asylum 49 performers themselves, who were well-versed in the art of standing totally still until a customer came within arm's reach, at which point they would suddenly leap forward and make a grab for them. Shrieks of terror that ultimately gave way to hysterical laughter usually ensued.

To make things a little more interesting, the second room was lit with a pulsing white strobe light, which gave the scene an even more bizarre and frightening appearance by making it appear as though the performers were jerking and twitching spastically.

On one particularly busy weekend evening, Asylum 49 happened to be short-staffed. Lacking one of the three performers that was usually placed in the room to portray an evil nurse, Cami Andersen gamely agreed to step in and play the role herself. She always enjoyed dressing up and getting her hands dirty alongside the other performers, and figured that this would be her chance to have a little fun.

Pulling on a white leotard and nurse dress and getting her makeup taken care of, Cami made her way to what everybody was now calling the "*Silent Hill* room," where she joined two other performers who were costumed in exactly the same way. Each one of them nodded in greeting at the others.

As the evening rolled along, it soon became apparent to Cami that the creepy nurses were turning out to be one of the Asylum's top scares that year. Group after group came through, but more than a few of them entered the room, caught sight of the nurses, and did an immediate about-face and left without even stepping foot inside. This was high praise indeed for the performers, although Cami wondered whether part of it might be due to the disconcerting effects of the strobe lights, which were well-known to make some people very uncomfortable indeed. It wasn't unknown for customers to complain of feeling nauseated after being exposed to their effects, which was why their use was restricted to very minimal levels at Asylum 49.

Those customers who had done a 180 in an attempt to evade the horror nurses were to find themselves out of luck, as the actors who were portraying the nurses would swiftly block the doorway, ushering them forward into the *Silent Hill* portion. For those performers, it was much more uncomfortable standing under the strobe lights for a prolonged period of time, and so they developed a routine of scaring each group of customers that entered their room, and then ducking outside for a bit of a break until the next bunch came along.

After terrifying the living daylights out of one hollering gaggle of customers, Cami and her two female colleagues ducked out of the room to await their next batch. Each of the girls was wearing a white body-suit, with a full mask covering their faces; the masks zipped up behind the back of the wearer's head, severely restricting visibility and making claustrophobia a constant companion.

Walking along at the very back of the line, Cami peered out through the two tiny eye-slits in her mask at the back of the actress in front. She was moving in an odd manner. Each step she took seemed to be stiff and labored somehow, as though it was a struggle for her simply to walk. The girl's head was tilted over toward her left shoulder at a bizarre angle that looked very uncomfortable to maintain.

Photo is taken with a fisheye lense of the Green Mile off of the main hall. The double doors at the end of the hall connect the hospital to the nursing home. Rooms 20 and 21 are down the hall on the left and the x-ray room entry is on the right.

Oh no, Cami found herself thinking, *the strobes are making her sick . . . we're going to lose another performer from the room tonight.*

Watching the girl slowly weave her way around the mannequins and furniture in a way that looked almost drunk, Cami became genuinely concerned that she would have to carry the actress out of the room and into the fresh air, so erratic had her gait suddenly become. Her motions became increasingly jerky and spasmodic with every step she took.

Looking around to make sure that the room was completely empty of customers, Cami verified that she was indeed the last person in the room. Turning back, she reached for the heavy black curtain that separated the two rooms from each other. Pulling it aside, she stepped through into the strobe-free environment, breathing in a deep sigh of relief.

Then she paused in her tracks. The other two girls were sitting there on the linoleum floor, chatting comfortably to one another. Their masks were off and they looked to have been in there for quite some time. More concerning, neither looked like the nurse she had just followed to the edge of the *Silent Hill* room. She had only turned her head away for a second to check the room, expecting the nurse in front of her to duck through the curtain into this room, but now that she thought about it, the curtain had been absolutely still when it was her turn to move it aside.

"Was there another nurse in there with us," a suddenly bewildered Cami asked, "or was it just us three?"

The two girls looked blankly at each other, then back at Cami. One of them said slowly, "Just us three," as though it was the most obvious thing in the world.

Had they seen another nurse step through the curtain before Cami? No, they had not. Yet Cami knew that the other woman—the one who had been jerking and twitching almost uncontrollably as she staggered—was directly in front of her, and had written it off to sickness caused by the strobe lights. Now she had to think again. Was there a rational explanation?

She asked the girls how long they had been out of the strobe-lit room. "A few minutes now," they told her, and neither had seen the figure that she had described. Had it simply been a figment of Cami's imagination? It's possible, she admitted, but she thought it unlikely. The nurse had been close enough for her to reach out and touch, and had seemed completely solid in appearance, no different from the two flesh and blood girls who had been keeping her company in there.

It was with some degree of reluctance that Cami returned to the *Silent Hill* room, her two colleagues in tow, to finish out their evening's work. She kept a constant eye out for the return of the mysterious phantom nurse, watching the shadows and darkened corners of the room in between bouts of leaping out upon the unsuspecting customers, but she didn't return that night, and hasn't been reported by any other observers since then.

This puzzling apparition is simply one of the many mysteries that make up the haunting of Asylum 49.

x x x x x

During a late investigation toward the end of their stay at Asylum 49, Richard and Sean teamed up with staff members Julie and Tyson in an attempt to gather a little more information about the haunting. They quickly settled upon what they thought was the best place to begin their experiments, and the four immediately headed toward the Green Mile and its surrounding areas.

The memory of the wooden door slamming was still fresh in Richard's mind. Each time that he passed it, he would look warily at it, making sure that the wedge was still firmly in place to keep it open.

The Green Mile branched off the main hallway in which that particular door stood, and it wasn't unreasonable to assume that any spirit that might have slammed it so forcefully behind Richard could also haunt the Mile and the cabin in the woods too, for that matter.

Richard couldn't help but be intrigued by the potential identity of whoever—or *whatever*—it was that had taken such a dislike to him the night before, and wanted to spend the evening trying to shed some more light on the situation. Was it perhaps the spirit of the authoritarian doctor whose apparition had been seen in the Emergency Room on multiple occasions? Or perhaps it was the ghostly nurse that haunted the Green Mile who had singled him out for a lesson in respect?

Worse still, could it actually have been the Guardian, seeking to frighten and intimidate the strangers from Colorado?

After a brief consultation, the four investigators agreed to try the Human Pendulum technique once again, having been impressed with the results that it had gotten them in the Nursery. Richard volunteered to go first, standing on the bottle-green carpet in the center of the Mile and asking any spirits present to show him his "yes" and "no" positions. They came straight away, tilting him forward for "no" and backward for "yes."

Recording with a high-definition camera, Sean kicked off the first bunch of questions with "Are you upset with the way that Richard ran the first ER [simulation]?"

No.

"Are you upset with how he spoke with the nurses?"

No.

Then came the question they had all been waiting for.

"Are you the one that slammed the door shut on Richard?"

There was no response. Richard simply stood there in the dark, trying not to breathe too noisily. He didn't move a muscle, simply standing there and silently willing the spirits to answer.

They didn't.

"Are you . . . is this Robert?" Tyson asked. *No.* "Is this Maria?" *No* again.

"Is this the Guardian?" Sean interjected. There was no response, so he changed tack slightly. "Are you mad at Richard?" *No.*

"Did you just want to scare him—is that why you slammed the door?" proposed Tyson. Richard began to feel himself moving backward. When Sean jumped in and asked whether it was more of a prank, the backward movement suddenly became more forceful.

"Was it Christian that slammed the door? Was it Jessica?" *No* to both. So, neither of the child spirits who were associated with the nearby chapel was to blame. Thinking back to his sighting on Halloween night, Richard decided to try a test question.

"Was it Jessica that I saw on Halloween night, leading that lady forward?" he asked.

No.

"Was it Sara?" Tyson asked. "Sara, was it you?"

No.

"Was it a living person that I saw?"

This time, the backward force was practically a shove—a most definite *no*.

Somewhere far off in the building, a door slammed. It seemed to come from within the general direction of the maze.

"Do you want us to go off to a different room?" Tyson wanted to know. When the answer came back in the affirmative, he began to list locations, getting told *no* until he finally asked whether the entity wanted them to go to where Maria was said to stand: *yes*.

The investigators duly trooped over to the section of the Mile in which several psychics have claimed to see Maria. Sean volunteered to become the subject of the experiment this time, and Richard gladly relinquished the spot to him. This time, Sean's "yes" was a backward move, and his "no" was to the right, directly toward where Richard was standing and filming him.

"Is Maria in this hallway right now?" Tyson took on the role of lead questioner.

Sean began to tilt backward. *Yes*.

"Close to us?"

No.

"Does she like us being in this hallway?"

Yes.

"Were you upset when Richard was doing that . . . *show* in the ER?" Tyson asked, referring to the cardiac arrest debacle of the night before. Sean found himself tilting forward, which was neither a "yes" nor a "no." Confused, Tyson asked for Sean to be shown his "no" position again; instantly he began to sway toward his right.

Clearing his throat, Richard asked if he was addressing Maria. The answer was a very clear *yes*, with Sean tilting back onto his heels.

"Maria, do you know that I'm a medical professional, like you are?"

Yes.

"Were you there when I was snapping at the nurses and the ER personnel?" Richard went on, fascinated at the possibility that he might be communicating with the spirit of a dead nurse via the medium of his friend's body.

Yes.

"Were you there when I apologized for it at the end of the night, and said that it was just a simulation?"

Yes.

"Have you forgiven me for that behavior?" he asked hopefully.

The answer was nothing short of bizarre. Rather than tilting backward, as Richard was hoping, Sean instead tilted forward onto the balls of his feet, but then proceeded to rock backward and forward several times. The investigators looked at one another in puzzlement. What the heck did *that* mean—"maybe," perhaps?

"Would you like me to apologize again?"

Sean continued to rock back and forth. Richard called out a request for him to be centered, which duly happened; Sean managed to find equilibrium again within seconds.

"Would you accept my apology now for what happened in the Emergency Room?"

Sean was pushed back forcibly enough that he struggled to keep from falling over—a definite *yes.*

"Is there somebody else in this hallway now," Tyson asked suspiciously, "somebody that's controlling Sean?"

Yes.

"Are you a doctor?" No response. "Are you a nurse?" Still no response. "Are you a . . . medical professional of some other type?"

Bingo. Sean stumbled backward.

"Did you take offence to the way I ran that cardiac arrest?" asked Richard. There was no response, but when Tyson asked whether the spirit used to treat its patient that way sometimes, the answer was a resounding *yes.*

"Did it invoke some unhappy memories for you?"

Yes.

"Do you like how the haunted house keeps the medical aspect alive?" Tyson was referring to the costume theme of demonic doctors and nightmarish nurses, along with the horde of monstrous medical assistants that frequented Asylum 49 every Halloween. Apparently, the unseen entity was a horror fan, because Sean was quite plainly pushed backward.

"Do you like having medical professionals around again this week?" put in Richard.

Yes.

"Do you wish this hospital was still open?" got no response at all, but "Are you an earthbound spirit?" garnered a *yes*, as did "Are you earthbound through your own choice?"

"Do you want to move on into the next world?" No sooner had Richard asked this than Sean was pushed forward, almost falling flat on his face.

Tyson asked whether the spirit was forced to remain in the old hospital because of something that it had done when it was alive, and received an immediate answer in the affirmative. Richard followed up by asking whether that "something" had taken place in this hospital, and was also told *yes*.

Were the investigators now witnesses to a confession?

"Do you regret what you did?" Tyson asked, getting no response. When he followed up by asking whether the spirit would do whatever it was again if it had the chance, Sean teetered backward again. *Yes.*

"Did it involve a bad patient outcome?" Richard had intentionally used the sanitized medical phrase that was sometimes employed when a patient died, or was horribly injured or sickened, when under the care of medical providers. Sean tilted forward once again, and reported to the group that he felt as though somebody was trying to lock his legs somehow, preventing them from moving.

The next question was "Would it help if we forgave you?" The answer was *yes*.

Speaking to the empty air, Richard asked if the spirit knew what EMTs and paramedics were. It did.

"Do you respect them?" Richard was now laying some groundwork; he was a paramedic, and Tyson was an EMT. Sean tipped backward, which pleased the two first responders greatly. "Would you like an EMT and a paramedic to forgive you for whatever it is that you did here?"

Nothing.

"Maybe they want a doctor to forgive them," Sean suggested, only half-jokingly.

The answers were becoming maddeningly inconsistent, and so the investigators decided to try a new approach. Still quietly observing the scene, Julie sat in a comfortable old armchair while Richard and Sean stood back to watch Tyson. Crouching in the middle of the Green Mile, the local investigator carefully set down a flashlight. Its bulb was completely dark.

"Alright, we know you can move Sean," he called out, stepping back to join Richard and Sean. "If you want us to leave, you've gotta turn this flashlight on."

Ten seconds later, the bulb began to flicker off and on. Nobody was within 15 feet of the flashlight.

"All the way on," Tyson insisted firmly. "If you want us to leave, then I want that bulb *all the way on*."

The light went out again, and stayed that way.

"Do you want me to come down there?" Tyson asked with a sigh. "Because if you do, I want you to turn that flashlight on before I count to four. One . . . two . . . three . . ." The flashlight flickered back to life once more—not all the way, as he had requested, but it certainly seemed to be trying. Was this just an electrical trick caused by the tiny amount of expansion and contraction that was going on around the bulb itself, or was it a spirit genuinely attempting to interact with the investigators?

As with so many other things where Asylum 49 is concerned, it could be taken either way.

13

Confronting the Guardian

Nothing says "haunted house attraction" quite like a maze, and Asylum 49 has several. All of them have their ghosts, and being situated on the darker side of the Green Mile divide, the paranormal activity that takes place inside them is never pleasant in nature.

Much as its name implies, the mirror maze is a series of cunningly designed corridors that are covered with reflective glass. There are switchbacks and dead ends galore. Navigating the mirror maze with the lights on is merely annoying, simply because the eye is easily fooled by the images of yourself that echo backward and forward into infinity on every turn; but turn out the lights and, with the introduction of a little smoke for atmosphere (which typically happens during the haunt), you suddenly find yourself in a part of the Asylum that is equal parts frustrating to escape from and terrifying to experience—particularly if you happen to be claustrophobic, or are just plain easily spooked.

Nor are you ever alone in the mirror maze, as a wolf-man silently prowls the corridors, looking for his next victim to stalk. Once the Asylum closes for the night and all of the performers have gone home, the maze becomes a hive of paranormal activity. More than one visitor has taken photographs in there which, although nobody was visible at the time, turn out to have

The beginning of the Guardian's territory, where Asylum 49's darkest, most violent activity is reported to take place.

mysterious background "extras" when the images are examined afterward. Hands, arms, and sometimes shadowy black figures tend to pop up as reflections in the mirrors. Some may be accounted for by pareidolia, the tendency of the human mind to want to find meaningful patterns in what is really just the random manner in which light falls on a reflective surface; yet others are not so easily explained away, particularly those that appear to be full-bodied human forms.

Situated at the rear of the x-ray room is one of the black mazes, so called because the room is filled entirely from floor to ceiling with black trash bags slashed into strips. Walking through such a maze is disorienting at the best of times, but once the factor of being sightless is added in, the maze becomes 10 times more frightening and sinister. Not only is it impossible to seem more than six inches in front of your face at any given moment, but the only sounds that can be heard are the constant rustling of something moving in the maze.

If you're really, *really* lucky, then the only thing moving in there is you.

Ghost hunts are now a long-established feature at the Asylum. In addition to providing a little extra income to support the restoration of the old hospital, paranormal investigators flock to Tooele in order to peek behind the scenes of the haunted house exterior in order to try and uncover some of the building's genuine ghostly secrets.

Misty Grimstead was participating in a ghost hunt inside the black maze late one night, when suddenly she felt two tiny hands—child-sized hands— grab her on each side.

"What the hell?" was the best that she could manage, before looking down and feeling her heart leap halfway out of her chest in terror. Two small red circles—a glowing pair of eyes—were looking straight up into hers.

She fled.

Nor is Misty the only person to have experienced physical phenomena in the black maze. A well-known local TV personality wanted to record a segment of documentary footage from inside the Asylum, and finally hit upon the black maze as the perfect backdrop for his needs. Misty guided him back into the maze and the pair commenced an EVP session for the benefit of the camera.

The reporter was suddenly *shoved* by a pair of invisible hands, with such force that once he had picked himself up, he immediately fled the hospital and refused to ever come back.

Several of the Asylum 49 staff members have observed that the majority of the dark, seemingly malevolent paranormal activity takes place on the south side of the building, just past the "Green Mile." The areas in and around the mazes seem to act as focal points for the more violent, negative entities and energies.

Of all of the spirits who haunt the Asylum, none is more frightening than the male entity who has been nicknamed "the Guardian." It would be tempting to think that based upon his nickname, the Guardian is the sort of spirit that is given to protect others; the mind conjures up images of a caring entity, perhaps looking out for the weaker souls at the hospital.

That interpretation couldn't be more wrong.

If the story of Asylum 49 has a true villain, then that villain is the Guardian.

x x x x x

On the evening of November 3rd, 2015, paranormal investigators Richard Estep and Sean Rice were the only researchers inside Asylum 49. Everybody else had gone home for the day, and the boys were locked in at their own request. The local school robotics club was holding a meeting down in the basement, but were asked not to come up onto the main floor, and very politely consented not to. As the night drew on, Misty dropped in to join the pair, something which had been agreed upon the previous day.

When discussing the experiments that would be carried out that evening, talk soon turned to the south wing, its mazes, and above all, the Guardian.

"We've heard a lot about him," Sean said. "He sounds like a total bully to me."

"He *is* a bully," replied Misty, and when asked to describe him further she ventured, "Quite honestly, he's just an *asshole*." She went on to explain that during his lifetime, the Guardian worked at the hospital in some capacity that isn't exactly clear—although the best guess is that he was an administrator, possibly some kind of assistant. No matter what professional capacity he worked in, however, she is convinced that he was most definitely "in the know" about a great many things . . . some of which were really none of his business.

Richard asked her whether this male spirit was simply misunderstood, or whether he really was essentially irredeemable. She replied that although he had suffered through some bad experiences during his physical lifetime, the way in which he treated people (particularly female visitors) was out of proportion to that and was totally indefensible.

The Guardian liked to know the secrets of others, she claimed, and hoarded them like cards to be played whenever it would work to his advantage. Knowing just who was involved with what dirty dealings gave him a power in life that was out of all proportion to his actual status within the hospital organizational structure.

By nature, this man was a coward and a bully, liking nothing more than to prey upon those who were weaker than himself—or at least were *perceived* to be. That may explain why he tends to target primarily women for physical attack and injury; although some males have been on the receiving end, the vast majority of the Guardian's attention seems to fall upon females.

Sean and Richard exchanged a meaningful look. Neither of them liked bullies. This sounded like a spirit that they would both very much like to meet. It took a little coaxing, but a patently nervous Misty finally agreed to escort them back into the recesses of the south wing—known throughout the Asylum as the Guardian's lair—to see whether he could be provoked into coming out of the woodwork.

The Boulder-based team of investigators usually does not believe in the use of provocation as a tool during paranormal research; after all, most provocation (by its very nature) involves behaving in a disrespectful way. Richard had stretched those boundaries to the point of discomfort during his cardiac arrest simulation in the Emergency Room, and although there had been some interesting results, the arrogant and aggressive way in which he had acted was still weighing heavily on his mind. The team was composed of respectful, compassionate people, and acting to the contrary went against the grain.

But *this* particular situation was quite different; based upon what they had just been told, the Guardian was hardly an entity that deserved a great deal of respect. He enjoyed terrorizing female visitors to the Asylum—just how would he cope with two big, brawny guys invading his personal space and getting in his face?

It took a little cajoling, but Misty finally agreed to guide the two investigators into the Guardian's territory for what promised to be something of a showdown. Misty explained that the Guardian was a very territorial spirit, and may react angrily and aggressively if he felt threatened on his own turf.

Consider, for example, the experience of security guard "Buck" Helige, Jr., who ran afoul of the Guardian's bad temper himself one night. It was at the height of the Halloween season, and Buck had been working hard all week. On this particular night, he was working security at the entrance to the black plastic maze.

During a rare moment of downtime, Buck found himself talking with one of his fellow staff members on the subject of the Guardian—the dark and angry spirit had been harassing staff members all week, claimed the other Asylum 49 employee, and it felt like it was getting a little out of hand. Buck frowned. He had seen the well-known shadowy form himself every single night of that week, and always in the same place: standing nonchalantly outside the doors to the prop store, simply hanging out and not causing any mischief.

"He doesn't seem to be up to much of anything when I see him," Buck mused thoughtfully, which earned him an *are you crazy?*-look from his colleague. As one of the few Asylum regulars who wasn't intimidated by the Guardian, he'd developed an attitude of "you leave me alone and I'll do the same for you" where he was concerned.

Later that night, after the haunt had closed and the staff had left, Buck ducked into the black plastic maze to make sure that it was empty. He had seen the Guardian enter the maze a few moments before, and then impatiently stick his head out when Buck hadn't followed right away. Figuring that *something* was on the cards, Buck walked with a little more care than usual, picking his way through the hanging plastic sheets.

What, he wondered, was the Guardian's game tonight?

Just as Buck was about to exit and turn toward the lab, he was shoved into the doorframe—not violently, but enough to send the very clear message that *somebody* wanted to make their presence felt.

Whirling around, the security guard could see that there was nobody around him; the hanging plastic strips weren't even moving, and there was no way a physical intruder could have concealed their presence from him.

Then the laughter started.

"The shove wasn't that hard," Buck clarifies, with the benefit of hindsight. "It was more of a '*just remember I'm here, and don't ever think I won't do something*' reminder."

A few months later, Buck was conducting a tour group around the former hospital and pointing out some of the highlights. While he was leading the way through the plastic maze, the security guard bumped into a solid figure in the darkness, somebody that seemed fairly big and sturdy.

Apologizing and working his way out to the exit, Buck heard one of the visitors call out from inside the maze and ask, "Buck, is that you?"

"No," Buck chuckled in reply, "but don't you worry . . . *I* ran into him too!"

And he has run into the mysterious figure on no less than four occasions, always while conducting his security rounds of the Asylum. Buck's standard approach is to simply acknowledge his presence, break contact, and go on swiftly about his business.

x x x x x

Armed with flashlights, EMF meters, and cameras, the trio made their way slowly toward the Green Mile, which seems to be the outer limit of the Guardian's area. Richard was wearing a firefighter's helmet with a hi-definition camera mounted to it, which he set to continuously record 1080p sound and video footage. Wherever he looked, the camera would record.

Bring it on, Estep thought to himself as the small group entered the "cabin in the woods" section of the haunt. He knew that they were securely locked inside the old hospital tonight, with security cameras keeping a watchful eye on all of the entrances and exits. Sean flipped off the lights every time they passed a switch, leaving the entire Asylum in a state of near-total darkness. Despite having spent the past 20 years investigating haunted houses on both sides of the Atlantic, Richard felt a very real sense of fear and foreboding run through him—a fear that grew with each step they took into the Guardian's domain.

The first odd thing to occur was the smell of smoke or fireworks. At first, Richard thought that it might have been an odor given off by his firefighter's helmet, which he had used on quite a few real fires before retiring it to make way for a newer one. Misty quite reasonably pointed out that they hadn't smelled anything like it further down the hallway, or back in the operations room when he had been carrying the helmet along with him, so why would it suddenly start smelling now?

"So what's causing it?" Sean asked, suspecting that he already knew the answer. The smell of smoke or burning inside the Asylum usually meant that Jeremy, its resident burn victim ghost, was lurking around. Richard doffed the helmet and offered it to Sean, who sniffed it tentatively. "Doesn't smell like anything," he concluded, ruling it out as the source of the smoky odor.

Pushing on deeper into the south wing, the small team made their way deeper, passing through corridors that were reminiscent of a wooden shack or homestead with military camouflage netting covering the upper walls and ceiling.

"*Please* don't lose me," Misty practically begged as she bravely led the way into the darkness, turning every few seconds to make sure that one of the investigators was right behind her and covering her six.

Richard wondered out loud why it was that the Guardian preferred to haunt this particular part of the hospital. Was it the sightless element? Did he enjoy stalking people in the cramped confines of the narrow, shadowy corridors and the claustrophobia-inducing maze interiors? Misty replied that yes, that was indeed the case—this part of Asylum 49 was an almost perfect hunting ground for a paranormal predator, particularly because even the most level-headed person began to feel the pangs of fear once they stepped inside and could no longer see.

The investigators reached the black maze, which slowed their pace further as even the tiniest vestiges of light were now gone, leaving them totally and utterly blind except for the flashlights each one carried. Each halting step forward required them to "swim" with their arms, slowly pushing aside the hanging trash bags with a wince-inducing rustle.

Pushing through the black plastic maze, the investigators made their way through more dimly lit corridors that were decked out like a forest trail, complete with a huge werewolf that was gnawing on the guts of a disembow-eled deer. They had to tread carefully, for fear of accidentally stepping on the pressure pad trigger that would cause the werewolf to lunge at them, powered by a pneumatic piston.

Navigating their way gingerly through the woodland-themed corridors, the trio decided to hold their investigative session in a room that was decorated in the style of Grandmother's house from the "Little Red Riding Hood" fairy tale. The room's centerpiece was a large bed occupied by a little old lady (in the form of a mannequin) who, unbeknownst to first-time visitors, was actually lying on top of a hollow mattress that contained another mechanical werewolf. When the correct switch was thrown, the top of the bed would be hurled upward, and a growling lycanthrope would rush up out of the dark pit below.

Fortunately for the three already-wary paranormal investigators, their furry roommate was currently switched off, and they only had to contend with the rather smug smirk of Grandmother, who seemed to be staring at them expectantly over the tops of her wire-framed spectacles.

Suddenly, Misty stopped dead in her tracks, followed seconds later by Sean and Richard. "Do you hear that?" she asked.

They all did. Somewhere, not so far away from them, they heard the heavy, measured tread of footsteps. They seemed to be coming from behind them, following the path that the investigators had taken already.

Oh crap, Richard thought to himself, his heart suddenly racing. *Something really is following us. It has to be the Guardian . . .*

When the team stopped moving, the footsteps stopped too. It felt almost as though whatever was making them was determined to move only when the investigators moved, masking the sound of its own footsteps by synchronizing them with the investigators' own movements. Closing up on one another instinctively, the team slowly took up positions facing the bed, each of them pressing their backs against the wall in order to get some sense of security, however false it may be.

"He's somewhere close," Misty said, her tone gaining an edge of trepidation. She looked pointedly toward the door that led to the mirror maze, one of the room's two exits. Finally, after drawing a deep breath, she invited the Guardian to come out and talk to them.

Sean reached out and killed the lights, while Richard turned on the Ovilus. *Eerie* was its first word, and the three of them couldn't have agreed more.

"We know all your secrets, Guardian," the psychic went on. "We know that you weren't a good person when you were alive."

Pulling out his camera, Richard began to take flash photographs, cautioning Misty and Sean first so that they would be able to close their eyes and preserve some night vision.

Redcoat, the Ovilus said, and then followed it up with the word *demon.*

"Do you think Richard's a redcoat demon?" Sean asked, suppressing a laugh. Richard's English heritage was a common source of humor on the team. The word *demon,* however, was a little more concerning.

Energy, said the Ovilus, and followed it with *king.*

Richard invited the Guardian to come and stand alongside him. Although he couldn't see anything himself, Misty maintained that the dark, angry spirit was clearly visible to her, and was hovering right next to him, before moving around to stand directly in front of him. She pointed out that the Guardian really didn't like him in the least.

"Aww," Richard pouted sarcastically, "why don't you like me, Guardian? Because I challenge you—is *that* it? Or is it because I talk funny?"

"He says that it's because *he's* the boss," Misty answered on the Guardian's behalf. "He thinks that you're trying to take over here."

Right, Richard thought to himself, *time to see whether we can get a rise out of this guy.*

"You're not the boss!" he began indignantly. "That's Kimm, Cami, or Dusty. *You're* not the boss at all. In fact, even when you were *alive,* you weren't the boss! You did what the doctors told you to, didn't you?"

The blackness seemed to grow more oppressive in the room, but the investigators acknowledged that it is entirely possible that this was purely psychological—after all, they reasoned, who *wouldn't* be nervous when standing in a dark room in the middle of a haunted hospital, with disembodied footsteps walking around outside and only a werewolf for company?

"We really need to check ourselves for scratches when we get out of here," Misty said, an anxious voice in the dark.

"I tell you what, Guardian," Richard was getting deliberately more belligerent now, bent upon provoking the aggressive entity into a response, "*scratch me.* No, please, scratch me if you don't like me. Go right ahead!"

The response was not exactly what he was expecting.

"Where are you going?" Misty sounded surprised. "He's leaving through that far door."

Sean heard what he swears sounded like footsteps coming from the same doorway, though none were picked up on the team's recording equipment.

"You're scared? Really? Of little old *us?*" Richard continued to taunt.

All three of them heard the footsteps this time, receding into the mirror maze.

"Richard wasn't backing down, so he ran," Misty explained. This had never happened before. Most people who challenged the Guardian tended to come off the worse for it, but like all bullies, when it finally came down to it, what was reputed to be Asylum 49's most terrifying entity had proven itself to be little more than a coward.

Misty explained that the Guardian was now hiding out in the maze area, eavesdropping on the three of them. She found his uncharacteristic behavior unsettling, being far more used to him going on the offensive where newcomers were concerned, rather than skulking in the shadows after somebody had confronted him directly.

Wanting to try a different approach, Sean asked the Guardian whether he had simply gotten a bad rap through the years, and if in fact the many rumors about his distasteful behavior during his physical lifetime were simply that: rumors.

"This is your opportunity to dispel any unfair rumors and to defend yourself," Richard offered, spreading his hands reasonably. "Perhaps you could restore your reputation. All you have to do is talk to us."

"He says *f—* you," Misty replied immediately. "He's screaming in your face, lots of profanity, literally just a few inches from your nose."

"Oh *really?* F— me, huh? Well, let me tell *you* something, mister . . ." Richard launched into a tirade, calling out the Guardian for his cowardly behavior. Although no foul language or cuss words were employed, the paranormal investigator left the Guardian in no doubt whatsoever as to the opinions he held of his behavior, particularly when it came to physically assaulting the female inhabitants of Asylum 49.

Misty reported that he was backing out again, more slowly this time, but still in retreat nonetheless. After the confrontation was over and he had been shouted down, the Guardian slunk away into the mirror maze (the team would hear footsteps coming from there for the next hour or so) and would not show his face again for the remainder of the investigation.

Their session in the Little Red Riding Hood room had raised as many questions as it had answered. For example, Richard wondered whether the Guardian was the entity who had scratched Autumn's back and shoulder following the spirit box session in and outside Room 666. That type of shockingly aggressive behavior toward a female visitor was certainly consistent with his *modus operandi*. Despite the commonly accepted wisdom at Asylum 49 that the Guardian never ventured any further afield than the log cabin located on the Green Mile, could it be that he was in fact responsible for Autumn's injury and for the aggressive, sexually suggestive words that had come through the spirit box?

It was certainly possible. Despite the Guardian's home turf being the mirror maze and the black plastic maze areas, there was no real reason for him to be confined to those parts of the hospital if he chose not to be. Had he been drawn to the energies of the paranormal investigators clustered around Room 666 that night, particularly given the fact that more than half of their number had been female?

Or was there an entirely separate dark entity haunting the hallway outside Room 666—an entity whose mind was set upon both verbally and physically abusing any female visitors who were brave enough to set foot inside its sphere of influence?

On the answer to this question, as with so many of the other mysteries associated with the haunting of Asylum 49, the jury is still most definitely out.

AFTERWORD

For every question that it answers, Asylum 49 has a maddening habit of raising a dozen more. As Richard and his teammates packed their bags before heading out on the long trip back to Colorado, their minds were teeming with unanswered questions.

Who exactly had slammed the door on Richard after the ER debacle?

What had influenced Sean's ever-sunny and upbeat mood, in both the Nursery area and the chapel?

Had Richard seen the apparition of a little girl on Halloween night, or was there some other explanation?

What was the identity of the dark, misogynistic entity that had spoken via the spirit box outside Room 666? Was it the spirit of Westley having a particularly bad night, or someone, perhaps some*thing*, else entirely?

And just who or what had scratched Autumn's shoulder?

These, and a host of other similar questions, ran through their minds as the team said goodbye for the final time that year, pausing in the parking lot for one last look back at the old hospital with its towering smokestack.

The next day, Richard and his investigators would go back to their everyday lives; but for the Andersens, the Lemmons, Dusty, Misty, Cathy, and the other regulars, it was already time to start planning for the 2016 Halloween season. Although the customers had stopped coming for the year, the ghost hunts would continue, as would the tours and the ever-present process of construction for the haunt.

Each night, when the building was locked up and abandoned, the resident spirits would still walk through its rooms and hallways. Jeremy, the great masquerader who always smells of smoke; Robert, the protector, and the children who he sometimes takes under his wing; not to mention the Guardian, who should now be happier at having the maze areas all to himself once more, and Westley, who would probably welcome a little peace and quiet in Room 666 after the breakneck pace of the past week.

All of them, and the rest of the Asylum 49 cast of characters, would have a little time and breathing room on their hands before the old hospital got busy once again.

Perhaps the most important question of all still remains mostly, but not entirely, unanswered: What does the future hold for Asylum 49?

The attached nursing facility is tentatively due to relocate elsewhere sometime in 2017, at which point the Asylum owners hope to acquire the entirety of the structure for themselves and incorporate it into the haunt. Many ghost stories are attached to that part of the building, which remains completely uninvestigated, an enticing mystery that no paranormal investigator worth their salt could possibly ignore.

Yes, Richard thought as he and Sean pulled out of the parking lot, they would be back. Asylum 49 had not given up all of its secrets yet, and he had a feeling that its story was only just beginning.

To view some of the photographs and EVPs mentioned in this book, please visit *www.asylum49.com/index2.html* or *http://www.richardestep .net/books/the-haunting-of-asylum-49/.*

INDEX

ABOUT THE AUTHORS

Richard Estep is a paramedic and training chief, who also serves as a volunteer firefighter in his adopted state of Colorado. He is director of the Boulder County Paranormal Research Society (BCPRS) and has spent the past 20 years investigating claims of paranormal activity on both sides of the Atlantic. Richard is the author of several books in the paranormal field, the most recent being *The World's Most Haunted Hospitals*. He has appeared in the TV show *Haunted Case Files*.

Cami Andersen is owner of the Old Tooele Valley Hospital, Asylum 49, along with her husband Kimm, niece Dusty Kingston, and sister-in-law Sonja Andersen. She has been investigating claims of paranormal activity in homes and businesses across Utah and the surrounding states for more than a decade, all the while continuing research into the mysteries of the spirits at the Old Tooele Valley Hospital. Cami leads a busy life with Kimm raising their children, mentoring the children of Tooele, overseeing scholarship programs held at the Asylum 49 Community Center, and working with her patients at the dental practice where she works part-time. Cami enjoys the guilty pleasures of horror movies, fantasy books, antique shopping, traveling with her family, and the occasional Comic-Con to satisfy her love of all things nerdy.